COMFORT FOOD

COMFORT
FOOD

HOLLY GARRISON

A DELL TRADE PAPERBACK

A DELL TRADE PAPERBACK

Published by
Dell Publishing
a division of
Bantam Doubleday Dell Publishing Group, Inc.
666 Fifth Avenue
New York, New York 10103

Design: Stanley S. Drate/Folio Graphics Co., Inc.
Illustrations: Ellen Gleeson

A Smith and Kraus Inc. Book

The trademark Dell® is registered in the U.S. Patent and Trademark Office.

ISBN: 0-440-50266-7

Reprinted by arrangement with Donald I. Fine, Inc.

Printed in the United States of America

Published simultaneously in Canada

May 1990

10 9 8 7 6 5 4 3 2 1

BVG

To my mother,
Virginia Prescott,
with thanks for her sugar cookies,
fudge, fried chicken,
and all the other friendly foods
of my childhood.

COMFORT FOOD (n): Certain distinctive foods that are reminiscent of childhood, adolescence, less complicated times, and "Mommy!" Occasional indulgence in these foods by adults is considered safer than drugs or alcohol and less expensive than compulsive shopping.

CONTENTS

ACKNOWLEDGMENTS

A cookbook, if it is interesting, accurate, and useful, is almost always the result of the efforts and talents of many people. This one is no exception.

Very special thanks to Carol Gelles for cheerfully testing, retesting, altering, and usually finding the best and easiest way to cook most of these recipes.

Also to Elizabeth Crow, Carole Horii, Cynthia Searight, Pam von Nostitz, Susan McQuillan, Helen Scott-Harman, and other coworkers at Gruner + Jahr, U.S.A., for their interest, support, and willingness to adjust their schedules in order to work with me when the book was in its final stages.

And to so many others who generously shared their thoughts, ideas, and recipes for favorite comfort foods.

Thanks, too, to the most tireless of my coworkers, my Macintosh computer, which uncomplainingly put up with its unmechanically and unelectronically inclined owner. And to my good friend Syndi Carney, who told me which buttons to push the times the Mac gave up on me.

Finally, to my dear and patient husband, Gerry Repp, who may never ever want another bite of lemon-meringue pie, and who enthusiastically ate comfort food, and "interesting" combinations thereof, at nearly any time of the day or night I put it on the table.

FOREWORD

Has there ever been a day so gloomy that some special, friendly food with seemingly magical powers couldn't make it better?

It may have been a bitter hot radish that gave Scarlett O'Hara the intestinal fortitude she needed to save Tara from the tax collectors and carpetbaggers, but on that oppressive August morning when the Yankees were within an inch of Atlanta and Melanie agonized with untimely labor pains, Scarlett pined for real coffee with sugar and thick cream.

Ms. O'Hara is one of a growing list of fictional, famous, and just plain people who admit that they frequently think about, and sometimes indulge in, a particular food or flavor that makes them feel better, and hardly a day goes by that a magazine or newspaper doesn't print the recipe for a rock star's, actor's, or politician's fondly regarded feel-good food.

Comfort foods can be as different as the people who eat them. For some it's a matter of plunking down enough money to buy a high-priced chocolate candy. Others will take or make the time to fry a pan of Mama's chicken. When we reach for comfort food what we're really doing, of course, is reaching for those halcyon childhood days when the sun always shone and we basked in the unconditional love of Mommy and Daddy.

Although there are a few fortunates who find a sour pickle soothing (not everybody was born with a sweet tooth or fat tooth, you know), most of us prefer something a mite more sinful. Traditional comfort food is generally high in refined carbohydrates, or fat, and often both. It is usually white or beige and requires little chewing. It is almost never chic or trendy. In truth, it is just about everything we are warned against eating nowadays. But as unstylish as comfort food may be, it seems unlikely that it will go out of style any time soon.

No one, least of all I, would encourage a daily consumption of nothing but so-called comfort foods. But most would agree that a little comfort food now and then isn't all that bad if eaten within the confines of an otherwise reasonably healthy lifestyle. And many believe that the gentle stroking provided by a moderate intake of comfort food far outdistances the harm it might do.

Researchers seem unable to decide if the benefits of comfort food are purely psychological, or physiological, or some of each. When we're feeling down-in-the-dumps and out of sorts and decide to eat a brownie, is there something in the chewy little bar that really does trigger our bodies into making us feel better? Or are we simply taking a little fantasy trip back in time to Granny's kitchen, seeking her authoritative assurance that all is well in these live-it-up, blow-em-up, anxiety- and panic-producing times we live in. Comfort food does, for whatever reason, promote feelings of serenity and well being, and just about no one would disagree that psychological harmony is the foundation for a healthy body.

In writing "Comfort Food," I made the interesting discovery that it isn't always necessary to *eat* comfort food to derive its benefits (although my husband and I did sit down to some pretty strange combinations of comfort food on many occasions). Often just thinking about, or writing about, or reading about, a favorite food, bringing its attendant memories, was enough to relieve the pressure of chapter deadlines.

My biggest anxiety about writing this book was *which* comfort foods to include. As it turned out, I needn't have worried. When I asked more than 200 people from every section of the country the same question, "What's your favorite comfort food?" the answers I got were always very much alike. Then I began to have the opposite worry: could I come up with enough *different* recipes. What I've tried to do is include those recipes that are generally considered to be all-time favorites of the "typical" middle-American family, circa the thirties, forties, and fifties—and just right for the eighties.

The recipes in "Comfort Food" were tested using the same kind of equipment (and under the same conditions) that I suspect most of you have available. I've tried to be specific about the ingredients; the only two assumptions are that you will use large eggs and lightly salted butter, except when otherwise specified. In all cases, margarine can be substituted for butter.

About the heart-preserver tips, I've attempted to healthy-up the recipes where appropriate, in case you just can't bring yourself to use those high-fat ingredients, even on rare occasions.

I doubt that you will ever cook every recipe here. If you're at all like me, you'll probably get a lot of pleasure and a few kicks from just reading and reminiscing. My fondest wish is that you will find as much comfort using the book as I did writing it.

COMFORT FOOD

I GRANNY'S GREATEST HITS:
Choice Pacifiers from
Sunday Dinners and
Other Big Events

Everyone has a mental picture (not always accurate, of course, but who cares) of the sweet-faced, twinkly-eyed little old lady with a heart of gold, a comfortable bosom, and a faded apron that seems permanently fastened to her flowered housedress. And just conjuring her up in your mind's eye on a bad day can make you feel better.

Usually flushed from the heat of the kitchen and beaming happily in anticipation of feeding her family, Granny didn't worry about words like cholesterol, hypertension, and, God forbid, calories.

Granny's big square kitchen, the focal point of her house, was almost as comfortable as she was, with wall-to-wall linoleum, an alcove for the icebox, and a profusion of African violets on the windowsill over the sink. (Granny swore she never did anything special for the violets; she just gave them a drink of water whenever she had one.)

Granny could cook like the dickens, and what we'd give right now to be sitting down to one of her never-to-be-forgotten Sunday-afternoon dinners.

Crisp Fried Chicken and Thick Skillet Gravy

Fried chicken is probably one of the most popular comfort foods. It is also one of the most controversial. How you fry yours (batter-dipped, deep-fried, pan-fried, coated with flour, coated with cornmeal, and so on) usually depends on where in the United States your Granny hailed from. My own grandmother came from Maryland, and her way to fry chicken was simply to dredge the pieces in flour and fry them in lard. (Most Grannies used lard for frying, you know, and as lethal a choice as that may seem by today's standards, nothing else even comes close to producing a fried chicken—or fried *anything*, for that matter—that is quite so golden brown, quite so crisp, quite so delicate, and quite so mouth-wateringly delicious. However, for the sake of your arteries, I'm suggesting a compromise: either substitute solid shortening for the lard or, if you care to take it one step further, substitute vegetable oil, peanut oil, or light olive oil for all or part of the lard.)

If she were around, Granny would give a lot of advice before you set out to fry your chicken. She would say that the secrets to perfect fried chicken are *time* and *patience*. While it's frying, chicken needs almost constant monitoring, frequent turning, and many heat adjustments under the skillet before it is, as they say, fried to a turn. So, if you'd rather spend your time before dinner gabbing and drinking, visit the Colonel or cook something else.

Granny would also tell you that it's easiest if the chicken is fried in one batch, which is usually too much for one skillet, unless you happen to have inherited her behemoth 12-incher. Two 10-inch skillets may be used simultaneously, which will make the frying job go that much faster. In that case, combine the drippings in one of the skillets to make the gravy. Or, you can use one skillet for frying and keep the cooked chicken warm in a very low oven, about 200°F. Finally, it is my sentimental belief that a well-seasoned, black iron skillet does the best frying job.

And one other bit of Granny advice before you begin: chicken frying is a spattery business, so do as she did and put a layer of newspaper on the floor by the stove while you're frying and there'll be no greasy floor to contend with the next day.

This is my Maryland grandmother's version of fried chicken, which, by the way, she would usually serve with little split biscuits as well as mashed potatoes. It is out of this world.

> 1 broiler-fryer chicken cut into 8 pieces (the back, broken in half, should be fried, too, because it makes great "picking" for those who enjoy the crispy part as much as the meat)
> Salt and pepper to taste
> 1 1/2 cups all-purpose flour
> 3/4 to 1 cup solid white vegetable shortening if using one large skillet, and about 1 1/2 cups shortening if using two smaller skillets.

> GRAVY
> Additional all-purpose flour, if needed
> 1 1/2 cups hot water
> 1 cup milk or water (yes, Granny used cream)
> Salt and pepper to taste

Rinse chicken pieces and place in a colander to drain thoroughly. However, the chicken should not be so dry that the seasonings and flour will not stick to it.

Sprinkle chicken rather liberally with salt and pepper, especially pepper. Place flour on a large piece of wax paper and dredge chicken pieces, one by one, placing them on a rack (the air circulating about them helps keep the coating in place) as you finish. Save the leftover flour for making gravy.

Melt shortening in a heavy, 12-inch skillet (or two smaller skillets as mentioned above) over medium-high heat. The fat should be at least 1/4 inch deep. When it is very hot, add the chicken pieces (the oil should *really sizzle* when the chicken is added), without crowding them, skin side down. (It's best to start with the dark-meat pieces, since they will take longer to fry. Wings and breast will cook more quickly.) Fry chicken pieces until golden brown, turning occasionally. It should take about 6 or 7 minutes to brown each side, so if the pieces brown too quickly or too slowly, adjust the heat down or up accordingly. When both sides are appetizingly colored; partially cover the skillet to allow the steam to escape and the chicken to finish cooking. Continue to cook, turning the pieces three or four times, for about 10 to 20 minutes, depending on the size of the piece and whether the meat is white or dark.

As the chicken pieces finish frying, drain them on paper towels and place on a platter. Put the platter in a 200°F oven where the fried chicken will keep very nicely until you are ready to serve it.

To make gravy, skim off most of the fat in the skillet, leaving a thin film. Make sure to also leave any browned particles in the skillet, for they will add a lot to the flavor of the gravy.

Place the skillet over medium-high heat until the fat sizzles. Stir in enough of the reserved flour to make a dry paste, or *roux*, as it's called. Lower heat and cook, stirring, until the flour mixture is medium to dark brown in color. Stir in hot water all at once (it will bubble and steam furiously), stirring until the mixture is reasonably smooth. Gradually stir in milk or water and continue to cook, stirring, until thick and bubbly. Add more water if the gravy seems too thick. Stir in salt and pepper to taste.

The gravy need not be served at once, but it will thicken some upon standing. Add a little more water or milk when reheating.

SERVES 4.

Heart-preserver tips: Fry chicken in vegetable oil and drain thoroughly on paper towels. Resist the gravy as much as possible.

Cure-You-Quick Chicken Soup

Probably the best known, most widely accepted comfort food, revered for its curative and restorative powers. Although some recent studies indicated that head colds treated with chicken soup did better than head colds that were not, most likely what makes us feel better when we eat this soup is the memory of being sick in bed and having Granny or Mommy catering to our whims and lagging appetites with steaming bowls of chicken soup, soft buttered toast, and dishes of trembly Jell-O. If you like, you can leave out the chopped carrot and celery in the final phase of preparation. The saffron, too, is optional, but a Pennsylvania Dutch touch that I simply cannot resist.

1 broiler-fryer chicken, weighing about 3 lbs., cut into pieces
3 or 4 celery ribs, including leaves, cut into pieces
1 large onion, cut into quarters
1 large turnip, rinsed, trimmed, and cut into quarters
1 large carrot, rinsed, trimmed, and cut into chunks
2 cloves garlic, peeled and quartered (optional)
1 large bay leaf
Few sprigs parsley
3 whole cloves
6 peppercorns
Few threads saffron (optional)
1 cup finely chopped carrot (about 2 medium)
1 cup finely chopped celery (3 or 4 ribs)
2 heaping cups uncooked medium-wide egg noodles
1 to 2 teaspoons salt
Chopped parsley for garnish

Rinse chicken pieces and place them in a large, heavy pot. (If you like, you can include the gizzard and heart, but not the liver, which you can freeze in a little container until you have collected enough of them to make Carol Gelles's Mother's Chopped Chicken Liver on page 110.) Cover with 12 cups of cold water and bring to a boil. Reduce heat and simmer, uncovered, for 30 minutes, skimming off the foam with a large spoon as it rises to the surface. Add celery pieces, onion quarters, turnip, carrot chunks, garlic (if using), bay leaf, parsley sprigs, cloves, peppercorns, and saffron (if using). When broth has returned to a simmer, cover and continue to cook for about 30 minutes, or until chicken is tender, but not quite falling from the bones.

Remove chicken pieces from broth with a slotted spoon to a platter. Cover the pot and allow the broth to continue to simmer.

When chicken is cool enough to handle, remove skin and bones and return them to the simmering broth. Cut chicken meat into small pieces (Granny used scissors to do this because they don't shred the meat.) Place in a tightly covered container and refrigerate.

Continue to cook the broth, covered, for 2 hours. Remove from heat and allow to cool slightly. Strain broth through a colander into a large bowl, pressing down hard with the back of a spoon to extract all the flavor from the solid ingredients. Discard residue in the colander.

With a large spoon, skim most of the fat from the top of the broth, or refrigerate and skim later after the fat has congealed. (Granny would say that it's important to leave about one-fourth of the fat in the broth for flavor.)

Return skimmed broth to cooking pot. Add chopped carrot and celery and bring to a boil. Stir in noodles and salt. Continue to cook at a slow boil until noodles are tender. Stir in reserved chicken and continue to cook only until the chicken is heated through.

Serve in large soup bowls, garnished with chopped parsley.

MAKES 6 SERVINGS.

Heart-preserver tip: Skim as much fat off the broth as you think you need to. Your heart, like the rest of your body, *loves* this soup!

Baked Pork Chops on Onion-and-Caraway-Seasoned Sauerkraut

The good news is that today's pork chops are leaner than ever, making them far less dangerous to your health. The bad news is that we wonder where the flavor went—and the tenderness and the juiciness—that anyone over the age of twenty-five remembers so well.

Granny's version of pork chops brings back some of the old-fashioned flavor of tender, browned pork chops, which, in turn, season the sauerkraut. If you don't care for caraway seeds (Granny always kept these on the shelf for rye-bread baking), leave them out.

4 loin pork chops, each about 1 inch thick
Salt and pepper to taste
All-purpose flour for dusting chops
1 tablespoon butter
1 medium-size onion, chopped (½ cup)
1 lb. fresh sauerkraut (as opposed to canned)
1 tablespoon caraway seeds, or to taste
¼ teaspoon pepper

Preheat oven to 350°F.

Trim excess fat from chops, reserving a few pieces. Sprinkle chops with salt and pepper to taste and dust with flour. (You don't want a heavy coating of flour; just enough to promote even browning.)

Place reserved pieces of fat in a large, heavy skillet. Heat, stirring, until the fat melts. (You should have about ⅛ inch of hot fat in the skillet.) Discard rendered fat. Place chops in the skillet and cook over medium-high heat until both sides are richly browned, turning the chops and adjusting the heat as necessary. Remove chops from skillet and set aside.

Wipe skillet with paper toweling and add butter. When it is hot, add onion and cook, stirring, over medium heat until onion is softened and just starting to brown. Remove skillet from heat and set aside.

Place undrained sauerkraut in a medium-size bowl. Add reserved onion, caraway seeds, and pepper, and toss until thoroughly mixed.

Spread sauerkraut mixture evenly in a shallow, 1½-quart baking dish that has been lightly greased or coated with nonstick spray.

Arrange browned chops over sauerkraut mixture and cover tightly.

Bake for 50 minutes. Remove cover and continue to bake for 10 minutes longer.

Granny would serve these chops with mashed potatoes (page 18) and applesauce (page 32).

MAKES 4 SERVINGS.

Heart-preserver tips: Trim all visible fat from chops and discard it; use a nonstick skillet and just a small amount of vegetable oil to brown chops, then onion; rinse sauerkraut with cold water to remove some of the salt, replacing the sauerkraut juice with water.

Chicken Stew with Light, Lumpy Dumplings

Granny knew that the better the chicken that went into it, the better the stew, so she used a "plump" roasting chicken instead of an old stewing hen in her version and so should you. A well-seasoned Dutch oven was her vessel of choice for stews, pot roasts, soups, and other recipes that required long, leisurely cooking, and maybe it was part of the reason they tasted so good. Lacking an iron Dutch oven, you can certainly use one of those excellent cast iron pots with the red, yellow, or blue enamel coating. The important thing is that the pot must be *heavy*.

1 roasting chicken, about 4½ lbs., cut into pieces (save neck and
    back for other uses)
3 tablespoons vegetable oil
4 cups hot water
1 medium-size onion, studded with 4 cloves
3 celery tops
5 large parsley sprigs
1 teaspoon salt
All-purpose flour for thickening stew
Coarsely chopped parsley or parsley sprigs, for garnish

DUMPLINGS:

2 cups all-purpose flour

1 tablespoon baking powder

½ teaspoon salt

2 tablespoons chopped parsley

¼ cup solid white vegetable shortening

1 cup milk

Rinse chicken pieces and pat dry on paper towels.

In a Dutch oven or other large, heavy stew pot with a tight-fitting lid, brown chicken pieces in hot oil over medium-high heat, removing pieces to a platter as they are browned.

Discard oil and wipe pot with paper towels. Return chicken to pot. Add hot water, clove-studded onion, celery tops, parsley, and salt, pressing the vegetables and chicken down into the water. Bring to a boil. Reduce heat and simmer slowly, tightly covered, for 1 to 1½ hours, or until chicken is fork-tender, but not falling from the bones. Remove chicken pieces to a platter and set aside.

Strain cooking broth into a 4-cup measure, discarding vegetables. Return broth to pot and skim as much fat as you want from the surface. (Granny would remind you at this point that at least *some* fat is necessary for flavor.) For each cup of broth, blend 1½ tablespoons flour and 3 tablespoons water to form a smooth paste. Gradually stir into broth. Simmer, stirring, until thick and reasonably smooth. Return chicken to thickened broth and set over medium heat to return to a slow boil while making dumplings.

To make dumplings, mix flour, baking powder, salt, and parsley in a large bowl. With a pastry blender or two knives, cut in the shortening until the mixture resembles coarse crumbs. (Just as a point of interest, Granny would have used lard instead of shortening for an even lighter dumpling, if you care to try it.) With a fork, lightly mix in milk to form a soft dough, stirring as little as possible.

Drop dough by the heaping tablespoonful (a serving tablespoon, not a measuring tablespoon) onto the chicken pieces in the now slowly boiling broth. Simmer dumplings *uncovered* for ten minutes, then *cover* and simmer 10 minutes longer.

If the occasion is very casual, you might want to serve the stew right from the Dutch oven at the table. Otherwise, arrange the chicken pieces on a serving platter and surround with dumplings. Cover lightly with thickened broth, serving the remainder on the side. Garnish with chopped parsley or parsley sprigs.

MAKES 4 TO 6 SERVINGS; 12 DUMPLINGS.

Heart-preserver tips: Pull skin and fat from chicken parts (except wings, which is practically impossible) before browning. Skim as much fat as you think you need to from the surface of the broth. Reduce salt to taste.

Tender Pot Roast with Potatoes, Vegetables and Pan Gravy with Horseradish Sauce

Everyone who ever ate it agrees that Granny's pot roast was never dry, never stringy, the reason probably being that Granny's beef, like her pork, was well marbled with fat, and yours can be, too, if you spend the money and buy your roast from a real butcher. He will sell you USDA Choice meat at the very least, or even Prime, if you're willing to spring for it—and it *will* make a difference.

If she could peer over your shoulder as you cook it, Granny would also advise you to brown the meat slowly and evenly, then cook it at just the barest simmer.

1 chuck or round-bone pot roast, about 1 1/2 inches thick, weighing about 4 lbs.

2 teaspoons salt

1/2 teaspoon pepper

All-purpose flour for dredging meat

3 tablespoons solid white vegetable shortening

1 large onion, chopped (1 cup)

1 cup boiling water

4 large carrots, scraped and cut into chunks

4 small turnips, peeled and cut in half

8 medium-size boiling potatoes, peeled and cut in half

1 lb. green beans, trimmed and cut into 1-inch lengths

GRAVY:

⅓ cup all-purpose flour
½ cup water
Liquid browning sauce (optional)
Salt and pepper to taste

HORSERADISH SAUCE:

1 cup sour cream
¼ cup mayonnaise
2 or 3 tablespoons well-drained prepared horseradish, the hotter
  the better

Sprinkle roast evenly with salt and pepper. Pat flour onto meat and set aside.

Heat shortening in a Dutch oven or other large, heavy stew pot with a tight-fitting lid. Cook onion in hot shortening over medium heat, stirring, until softened. Remove with a slotted spoon and set aside.

In the fat remaining in the pot, brown meat well on all sides, adjusting the heat as necessary. This may take a few minutes. Don't rush it!

Return onion to pot. Pour boiling water around roast. Adjust heat so that the liquid around the roast barely simmers. Cover and cook for 2½ to 3 hours, turning the roast once after 1 hour's cooking time and basting occasionally with pan juices until the meat is fork-tender.

About 1 hour before meat is done, add carrots and turnips, turning to coat with pan juices. About 30 minutes later, add potatoes and green beans, basting and pushing them down into the pan juices. Continue to cook slowly until vegetables are tender.

Remove roast to a serving platter and surround with vegetables. Cover with foil and keep warm in a 200°F oven while making gravy.

If very much fat rises to the surface of the liquid left in the pot, you may want to remove some of it with a large spoon before making gravy. (But remember what Granny says about some fat being left for flavor.) Beat flour and water in a small bowl until thoroughly blended and free of lumps. Stir into pot with a wire whisk. Cook, stirring, over medium heat until thick and bubbly. Continue to cook, stirring occasionally, for 2 or 3 minutes. If you want a darker gravy, add a few drops of liquid browning sauce. Season to taste with salt and pepper.

To make horseradish sauce, mix sour cream, mayonnaise, and horseradish in a small bowl. Scrape into a serving bowl and chill until ready to serve. This may be done several hours in advance.

MAKES 8 SERVINGS; ABOUT 2½ CUPS GRAVY; 1¼ CUPS HORSERADISH SAUCE.

Heart-preserver tips: Use a lean roast and trim away all visible fat before browning in vegetable oil instead of shortening. Wipe pot with paper towels after browning. Use vegetable oil for cooking onion. Skim all fat from surface before making gravy. Use reduced-fat sour cream and reduced-fat mayonnaise in the horseradish sauce.

Chicken-Fried Steak with Cream Gravy

If your family tree has its roots in the Southwest, it's quite likely that chicken-fried steak is one of your comfort foods. The method for making this steak and gravy is a lot like frying chicken. It's easy to understand how this old favorite sprang up in cattle country, where it used to be easier to get a cow than a chicken. Ranch Grannies used tough pieces of beef for chicken-frying, tenderizing them by pounding the meat with the dull side of a meat cleaver. You can save yourself from this noisy chore by using cube steaks that are already tenderized.

4 tenderized cube steaks, about 6 oz. each
½ cup milk
Salt and pepper to taste
½ cup all-purpose flour
1 egg, lightly beaten
¼ to ⅓ cup solid white vegetable shortening
½ cup whipping cream

Place steaks in a large, shallow dish (a baking dish works well) with the milk. Turn to coat each steak and set aside for about 1 hour.

When ready to fry, remove steaks and pat dry on paper towels, reserving the dish of milk.

Season steaks generously with salt and pepper. Lightly sprinkle each steak with some of the flour and pat into the meat.

Beat egg with milk remaining in dish. Sprinkle remaining flour on a piece of wax paper, reserving 2 teaspoons for gravy. Dip steaks into egg mixture, then dredge lightly in flour.

Heat shortening in a 10-inch skillet. When it is hot, fry steaks on both sides until golden brown, about 4 or 5 minutes per side. Remove from skillet to a warm serving platter.

Pour off all but a thin film of fat from the skillet, making sure to leave behind any browned particles. Place skillet over medium-high heat. Stir in reserved flour. Add cream and cook, stirring, until thick and bubbly. Season to taste with salt and pepper.

Serve each steak with a spoonful or two of the gravy. A mound of mashed potatoes (page 18) with a crater of melted butter and three-bean salad (page 93) should be served on the side.

MAKES 4 SERVINGS.

Heart-preserver tips: Reduce the size of each steak to 3 or 4 oz. Fry in a nonstick skillet with a minimum of vegetable oil. When making gravy, increase flour to 2 tablespoons and substitute low-fat milk or water for cream.

A Fat Roast Chicken with Buttery Bread Stuffing

Once upon a time, a plump roast chicken for Sunday dinner was the ultimate symbol of prosperity and well-being in America. How bad could things be when we were surrounded by a loving, happy family seated together at the big dining room table so loaded with serving dishes, platters and plates of food that the tablecloth was barely visible? Besides the chicken, Granny's Sunday dinners usually consisted of four or five vegetables, bread, rolls, relishes and condiments, hot and cold drinks and at least two desserts—an abundance of food that would nowadays be served only on one or two holidays a year, if even that often.

The chicken that Granny roasted probably had to scratch for its dinner, supplemented by handfuls of corn and other goodies that were believed to produce a fat, tender chicken. Granny had a good deal more cleaning and plucking to do than we do today, to make her chicken pan-ready, and when the bird was finally groomed to her exacting standards, she usually filled it with a stale-bread stuffing that was liberally laced with butter and poultry seasoning. More exotic stuffings (oyster, chestnut, and fruit stuffings, for example) were reserved for holiday dinners.

1 roasting chicken, weighing about 6 lbs.
Salt and pepper
Softened butter

STUFFING:
12 slices white bread, dried (see note)
1 medium onion, finely chopped (½ cup)
3 ribs celery, finely chopped (about 1 cup)
¼ cup chopped parsley
1 teaspoon poultry seasoning, or to taste
½ teaspoon salt, or to taste
¼ teaspoon pepper
1 egg, lightly beaten
4 tablespoons butter, melted
Warm water

Remove neck and giblets from chicken and set aside. Rinse chicken and pat dry inside and out with paper towels. Chill chicken until ready to stuff.

Place neck and giblets (except liver, which may be added to the collection of frozen livers you keep in the freezer in a tightly covered container until you have enough to make Carol Gelles's Mother's Chopped Chicken Liver on page 110). Cover by a couple of inches with cold water. Season with salt and pepper and bring to a simmer. Cover and cook slowly for an hour or so to make a broth for the gravy.

Break bread into postage-stamp-size pieces in a large bowl. Add onion, celery, and parsley and toss to mix thoroughly. Sprinkle with poultry seasoning, salt, and pepper, and toss again to mix well. Add egg and mix again. Drizzle with melted butter and mix again. Slowly add warm water, a tablespoon or so at a time, tossing until the bread is very moist, but not dripping or the stuffing will be gummy after it is cooked.

Preheat oven to 325°F.

Form stuffing into small, loose balls and lightly stuff the body and neck cavities of the chicken. Stuffing expands as it cooks, so don't pack the bird too tightly. Fold neck skin under the chicken and twist wing tips behind back. Skewer cavity closed and lace with kitchen string. Tie drumsticks together. If you like, you can insert a meat thermometer in the thickest part of the thigh. Place chicken on a greased rack (this will help keep the chicken from sticking after it is roasted) in a shallow roasting pan. Smear chicken with softened butter.

Bake for 2 to 2½ hours, basting the chicken every 20 minutes or so, first with the broth from the giblets and then with the pan juices as they start to accumulate. If the breast is brown before the end of the roasting time, shield it with a loose tent of aluminum foil. Test for doneness the way Granny did it: push a metal skewer into the thickest part of the thigh. If the juices run clear, it's done. If not, continue roasting and repeating the skewer test at 10-minute intervals. If you have used a meat thermometer, it should register 180°F.

Remove roasting pan from the oven and transfer the chicken to a platter to rest (this allows the juices to retreat into the meat and results in a juicier bird that is easier to carve) while making the gravy. Remove rack from roasting pan.

For *each cup* of gravy you will need to reserve about 1 tablespoon of fat. Pour off and discard remaining fat from roasting pan. For *each cup* of thick gravy you will also need 2 tablespoons of all-purpose flour and 1 cup of liquid (water, vegetable-cooking liquid, or the broth from the giblets, for example). If you prefer a thinner gravy, use only 1 tablespoon of flour per cup. Thoroughly mix flour and liquid in a small bowl. Place roasting pan over heat (you can set it across two burners if the pan is too big for one burner) and when the fat in the pan is sizzling, stir in the flour mixture with a wire whisk. Cook, stirring (be sure to stir up all the little brown pieces that cling to the pan), until thick and bubbly. Continue to cook for 1 or 2 minutes. Season to taste with salt and pepper. If you are adding giblets to the gravy, chop them into small pieces and stir into the gravy. You may just leave the gravy in the pan until you're ready for it at this point. Reheat just before serving, stirring in a little more liquid if the gravy has thickened while standing.

MAKES 6 SERVINGS

Note: To dry out bread (for this stuffing it should actually be *hard* when it is broken up), spread out on baking sheets or wax paper for about 24 hours, turning occasionally. You can also put the bread in the oven at the very lowest-setting for an hour or so, turning frequently until it is dry.

Heart-preserver tips: Do not butter skin; substitute chicken broth for butter in the stuffing; eat just one bite of the delightful, crisp-roasted skin.

Mashed Potatoes, Lumpy and Smooth

Little bits of unmashed potato signal "homemade!" to many of us, distinguishing them absolutely from the flavorless, instant variety that would have horrified Granny. Others of us like our potatoes mashed to a baby-foodlike consistency. As with most food, it all depends on what you grew up with. Granny would caution that if you overbeat your potatoes they will get sticky. And, once mashed, don't cover them or the condensation that forms on the lid will make the potatoes mushy. Granny would also have told you how important it is to use the right kind of potato for mashing. Use "general-purpose" or "boiling" potatoes, those brown, nondescript ones in the bin at the supermarket.

> *8 medium-size, general-purpose potatoes (about 3 lbs.)*
> *4 tablespoons butter, softened (you can, of course, use more)*
> *¾ cup milk (you can use light cream or half-and-half, and some*
> *Grannies preferred evaporated milk)*
> *½ teaspoon salt, or to taste*
> *⅛ to ¼ teaspoon pepper, or to taste*

Peel potatoes and cut into quarters. Cover by about 2 or 3 inches with lightly salted, cold water in a large saucepan. Bring to a boil. Reduce heat, cover, and boil slowly for about 20 minutes, or until potatoes can be easily pierced with a fork, but are not beginning to fall apart. Drain thoroughly. Add butter to the hot potatoes in the saucepan.

If you like lumpy mashed potatoes, mash with a potato masher until nearly smooth. Gradually add milk, beating with a table fork until the potatoes are the consistency that you like. Beat in salt and pepper.

If you like smooth mashed potatoes, do the whole mashing job with an electric hand-held beater set at medium speed (or a rotary beater like Granny used).

Turn into a warm bowl and serve immediately. If the potatoes are not to be served the moment they are mashed, they may be reheated by setting the pan over very low heat and beating until hot. Do not cover at any time after beating!

MAKES 6 SERVINGS

STOP! In the unlikely event that there are leftover mashed potatoes, don't throw them out. Mashed-potato cakes are a wonderful accompaniment to any meal, and once you've tasted them you'll always make sure you mash more potatoes than you'll need.

Chill leftover mashed potatoes. Shape cold mashed potatoes into flat, hamburgerlike patties. Dust with flour and sauté in butter, bacon drippings, or vegetable oil until nicely browned on both sides. If you want to take the cakes one step further, you can add lightly sautéed onion and/or green pepper to the cold potatoes before you form the patties.

Heart-preserver tips: Reduce or omit butter; substitute skim or low-fat milk for whole milk. Reduce salt to taste.

And, as long as we're on the subject, here's

How to Bake a Perfect Potato

Do not oil, wrap in foil, or do anything else to a potato you expect to be perfectly baked. A perfectly baked potato should have a dry, slightly chewy skin, and the inside should be moist and fluffy.

Use a Russet or nicely shaped general-purpose potato for baking and choose potatoes of similar size so they will bake in the same amount of time. Wash the potato under running water. If it is especially muddy, scrub lightly with a vegetable brush.

With the tines of a kitchen fork, pierce the potato two or three times. This prevents steam from forming inside the potato, which, at best, will tend to keep it from baking up dry and fluffy, or, at worst, exploding in the oven.

Place the potato directly on the oven rack and bake in a preheated, 400°F oven for about 60 minutes, or until the potato feels soft when lightly squeezed with protected fingers.

Slash a 1½-inch cross in the top of the potato, then gently squeeze both ends until the snowy-white interior partially bursts through the cross. Serve *immediately* with the topping of your choice.

By the way, potatoes can be baked at lower or higher oven temperatures to accommodate other dishes in the oven. In that case, for each 25 degrees lower than 400°F add 10 minutes of baking time. Potatoes may also be baked at a slightly higher temperature, say 425°F. In that case, reduce baking time by about 15 minutes.

Better Than Creamed Spinach

Better than what? Better than frozen creamed spinach, a convenience food that would have bowled Granny over, that's what! Indeed, many of her grandchildren would be greatly surprised to learn that there really was creamed spinach before it came in a boilable plastic, cooking pouch in a green box.

Granny often creamed her vegetables, for she knew if she did they'd stand a far better chance of being eaten. If you like, you can use the cream sauce here for other vegetables (celery, tiny onions, peas, carrots, or whatever you fancy) and it really makes them special.

If a bowl of creamed spinach with a big pat of butter melting on top (and a lamb chop on the side, perhaps) makes you feel like all's right with the world, you should treat yourself to this from-scratch version one day soon.

Wash the fresh spinach leaves like Granny did, in an immaculately clean kitchen sink in several changes of cold water to remove all traces of the sand that inevitably lurks in the leaves. If you want, you can even substitute frozen whole-leaf spinach and the finished version may still be the best you ever ate.

*1¼ lbs. fresh spinach or 2 packages (10 oz. each) frozen
    whole-leaf spinach
3 tablespoons butter
1 small onion, minced (¼ cup)
1 heaping tablespoon all-purpose flour
¾ cup half-and-half or light cream
½ teaspoon salt
⅛ teaspoon pepper
Pinch ground nutmeg*

Rinse spinach leaves in several changes of cold water. Remove tough stems and place leaves in a large pot with only the water that clings to the leaves. Cook over medium-high heat until spinach has wilted and is just cooked through. Drain in a colander, then squeeze to remove as much liquid as possible. (If using frozen spinach, cook as package directs, but only until spinach is hot. Proceed as with fresh spinach.)

Place spinach in the container of an electric blender or food processor and blend until finely chopped (but don't get carried away and puree it), scraping down the sides of the container with a rubber spatula once or twice. Set aside.

Heat 2 tablespoons of the butter in a medium-size saucepan. Add onion and cook, stirring, over medium heat until softened. Stir in flour. Add half-and-half all at once, stirring until mixture is thick and smooth. Stir in salt, pepper, and nutmeg. Add reserved spinach and continue to cook, stirring, for 2 minutes. Remove from heat and swirl in remaining 1 tablespoon butter.

MAKES 4 SERVINGS

Heart-preserver tips: Use margarine or substitute vegetable oil for 1 tablespoon or all of the butter when cooking onion; omit final butter addition.

Baked Mashed Sweet Potatoes with Melted Marshmallows on Top

Rarely was a ham served at Granny's (or anyplace else at one point in our nation's history) that this family favorite didn't come right along beside it. This is the original, unadulterated version of a great comfort food. It is light, smooth, and not too sweet.

As a point of interest, sweet potatoes and yams are botanically very different, but cooks have long known that the two can almost always be used interchangeably.

3 medium-size sweet potatoes or yams (about 8 oz. each)
½ cup half-and-half
¼ cup firmly packed, light brown sugar
2 tablespoons butter
½ teaspoon salt
2 eggs, separated
20 regular-size marshmallows

Cook sweet potatoes in boiling water until tender, about 40 minutes, and drain. When the potatoes have cooled slightly, peel them and return them to the cooking pot. Beat potatoes until they are smooth. (By the way, if you'd like to beat in a couple of tablespoons of butter and salt and pepper to taste, you can stop right here with perfectly comforting results. For an au courant touch, you could also add a teaspoon or so of minced, fresh ginger root.)

Preheat oven to 325°F.

In a small saucepan, heat half-and-half, sugar, butter, and salt over low heat, stirring, until butter has melted. Beat egg yolks in a medium-size bowl. Gradually beat in half-and-half mixture. Gradually beat egg-yolk mixture into potatoes.

Beat egg whites in a grease-free, medium-size bowl with clean beaters until stiff peaks form when beaters are lifted. Fold beaten whites into the potato mixture. Turn into a 1½-quart, buttered casserole. (May be refrigerated at this point and baked later.) Arrange marshmallows on top.

Bake for 25 to 30 minutes (longer if refrigerated before baking), or until marshmallows are melted and lightly browned and the mixture is heated through.

MAKES 6 TO 8 SERVINGS.

Heart-preserver tips: This is fairly healthy comfort food. But, if you wanted to, you could substitute milk for the half-and-half and soft margarine for the butter; leave out one or both of the egg yolks.

Best-Ever Corn Fritters

I have always considered these to be comfort food ever since they helped cure a bad case of homesickness my first time away at summer camp, and they have never failed me since. When I returned from camp, I described these fritters to my grandmother and they were sitting on a plate in front of me in less than 20 minutes. This is the first time I was aware that my granny didn't use cookbooks.

I must admit that I like my fritters in a pool of warm syrup, sometimes with a slice or two of thick-sliced, crisp-cooked bacon on the side.

1 cup all-purpose flour
2 tablespoons sugar (see note)
1 teaspoon baking powder
1 teaspoon salt
2 eggs
¼ cup milk
2 teaspoons vegetable oil
1 can (16 to 17 oz.) whole-kernel corn, drained
Vegetable oil for frying
Confectioners' sugar for dusting fritters
Warm syrup

Mix flour, sugar, baking powder, and salt in a medium-size bowl with a wire whisk until light and thoroughly combined. (Using a wire whisk to blend the dry ingredients makes sifting unnecessary in this case.)

Beat eggs with milk and 2 teaspoons of the vegetable oil in another medium-size bowl. Gradually beat in flour mixture, then stir in corn.

Pour vegetable oil for frying into a large skillet to a depth of 1½ to 2 inches. Heat to 365°F on a deep-fat thermometer. (You can use an electric skillet, which makes the frying a whole lot easier, but so few people own them these days.) Drop fritter batter by the serving tablespoonful into the hot fat. Do not crowd. Fry for 2½ to 3 minutes, turning only once, until golden brown. Remove to a wire rack that has been covered with two or three layers of paper towels to absorb excess oil. Every now and then, scoop out any small pieces of fritter batter left in the oil to keep them from burning. Keep fritters warm in a 200°F oven while frying successive batches.

Serve fritters warm, sprinkled with confectioners' sugar. Pass a pitcher of warm syrup.

MAKES ABOUT 14 TO 16 FRITTERS.

Note: Fritters made without sugar may be served as a vegetable side dish.

Heart-preserver tip: Eat just one or two small fritters—and not very often.

Scalloped Tomatoes

Because of their high acidity and the way they have always pro-
liferated in home gardens, tomatoes were one of the easiest and first
vegetables for home canners to preserve. Granny made the most of the
bushels and bushels of tomatoes from her garden. Some of the tomato
put-ups we remember on the shelves in her cool, dirt-floor basement
were chili sauce, catsup, stewed tomatoes, tomato juice, and just plain,
whole tomatoes. Scalloped tomatoes, which everyone loved, made
frequent appearances on the table, another one of Granny's innovative
uses for less-than-fresh bread.

2 tablespoons butter,
1 medium-size onion, chopped (1/2 cup)
2 cans (15 to 16 oz. each) whole tomatoes, drained
1 to 3 teaspoons sugar
1/4 to 1/2 teaspoon salt
1/4 teaspoon pepper
4 slices dry (but not hard) bread spread with softened butter and
*   cut into 3/4-inch squares (see note)*

Preheat oven to 350°F.

Melt butter in a large saucepan. When it is hot, add onion and
cook over medium heat, stirring, until slightly softened. Add drained
tomatoes and continue to cook until bubbling, stirring and breaking up
the tomatoes with the side of a spoon. Stir in 1 teaspoon of the sugar,
1/4 teaspoon of the salt and pepper. Taste and add more sugar and salt,
if you like. The sugar-salt ratio here is a very personal matter, but it
should be on the sweet side.

Spoon half the tomato mixture into a buttered, 1 1/2- to 2-quart
casserole or souffle dish. Arrange half the bread over tomatoes. Repeat
these two layers.

Bake for about 25 minutes, or until bubbling at the edge and
breadcube topping is lightly toasted.

MAKES 4 GENEROUS SERVINGS.

Note: The bread should be dry, but not hard. Spread fresh bread out on a piece of wax paper, turning once or twice for a couple of hours.

Heart-preserver tips: Substitute vegetable oil for butter when cooking onion. Go light when buttering the bread, or only butter two slices of bread and use them for topping the casserole.

Summer Corn Pudding

Like tomatoes and everything else in Granny's garden, sweet corn abounded. Most of it was eaten straight off the cob, of course, but every now and then Granny would vary the menu a little and serve this fabulous corn pudding. It's so good that maybe you, like I, will occasionally make this on a bleak winter's day, substituting canned creamed corn for fresh corn, and pretend it's summer.

12 to 16 medium-size ears sweet corn or 2 cans (17 oz. each)
    cream-style corn
2 eggs, beaten
2 tablespoons all-purpose flour
1 to 2 tablespoons sugar (depending on how sweet your corn is)
1 teaspoon salt
½ teaspoon pepper
4 tablespoons butter, melted

Generously butter a 1½- to 2-quart casserole with a lid.

Remove husks and silk and rinse corn.

To make fresh creamed corn, cut down the center of each row of kernels of one ear of corn with the tip of a paring knife. Stand corn upright in the bottom of a deep, wide bowl. Steadying the ear with one hand, with the *dull side* of the paring-knife blade, scrape down the ear (don't cut), releasing only the pulp and milky juices from the rows of cut kernels. Stand the ear on its other end and scrape again. Repeat with remaining ears of corn. You will need 3 to 4 ears of corn for each cup of corn pulp, and for this recipe you will need 4 cups.

Preheat oven to 350°F.

Add eggs, flour, sugar, salt, pepper, and butter to corn pulp (or canned corn) in a large bowl and mix thoroughly. If the corn is young and especially sweet, very little sugar will be needed. If using canned corn, you may want to omit sugar altogether.

Turn corn mixture into prepared casserole. Cover tightly (you can use foil if the casserole lacks a lid) and bake for 1 hour and 15 minutes, or until set in the center and a crust forms around the edge.

MAKES 6 SERVINGS.

Heart-preserver tip: Reduce melted butter to 2 tablespoons.

Granny's Never-Fail Method for Boiling Corn on the Cob

Granny had a tall case clock in the downstairs hall that used to chime on the hour, but she didn't own a kitchen timer, so it would have been impossible for her to follow the complicated timing directions that most cookbooks give for cooking corn on the cob. Her old-fashioned method never fails and makes cooking and serving corn on the cob much less of a hassle. Here's how she did it:

Bring a large pot of water to a boil. Don't put salt in the water because that will toughen the corn, Granny used to say. However, she did add a tablespoon or two of sugar to the water, presumably to sweeten the corn. When the water comes to a furious boil, drop however many ears of freshly shucked corn you plan to cook into the pot, at which point the water will stop boiling. Immediately put a tight-fitting lid on the pot and wait for about 1 minute. Turn the heat off under the pot and leave it, covered, for about 10 minutes. Remove the first servings of corn from the pot. Leave the rest of the corn in the covered pot. As the corn is eaten, simply continue to retrieve one or more ears from the covered pot as needed.

That's all there is to it, and you'll be amazed that every serving of corn is hot, tender, and not the slightest bit overcooked.

The only instance in which I cannot imagine this system working perfectly is if you are planning to have a real crowd over for a corn feast. In that case, you would probably need several pots of corn and you would want to stagger the cooking.

Iceberg Lettuce (Wedges or Shreds) with From-Scratch Russian Dressing

Many of us would never have believed as children that there was any other kind of dressing. Or any other kind of lettuce, for that matter. Granny, catering to our whims, as always, served her Russian dressing on iceberg-lettuce wedges, or sometimes iceberg-lettuce shreds for those of us who were too lazy to cut up the wedge and left it sitting naked on the plate after we'd scraped off the dressing. Russian dressing can be as plain as mixing catsup and mayonnaise to taste, or you can add little bits of olive, pickle, relish, crumbled bacon, garlic, green onion, or whatever strikes your comfort chord.

1 head iceberg lettuce
1 cup mayonnaise
¼ to ⅓ cup catsup
¼ teaspoon garlic powder
⅓ teaspoon pepper

Rinse lettuce head and drain thoroughly.

To make lettuce wedges, cut lettuce head into quarters through the core. Cut the core out of each quarter with a small paring knife. Chill until ready to serve.

To make lettuce shreds, cut lettuce head into quarters through the core. Cut the core out of each quarter with a small paring knife. Place each lettuce quarter, cut side down, on a cutting surface. Starting at the core end, cut the lettuce into very thin slices, at which point it will fall into shreds. Place shreds in a bowl and fluff with your fingers. Chill until ready to serve.

To make dressing, mix mayonnaise, catsup, garlic powder, and pepper in a small bowl. Chill until ready to serve.

To serve, place lettuce wedges or shreds on individual salad plates and spoon dressing over.

MAKES 4 SERVINGS; ABOUT 1¼ CUPS DRESSING.

Heart-preserver tip: Substitute reduced-fat mayonnaise for regular mayonnaise, or plain yogurt for some of the mayonnaise.

Old-Fashioned Potato Salad

Toss the potatoes with the other vegetables, the mayonnaise, and the seasonings while the potatoes are still warm, Granny would have advised the novice potato-salad maker. That way they absorb these flavors more readily and make the difference between a good potato salad and a great potato salad. Granny would also have told you to toss the salad very gently so the potatoes won't break or crumble. But if you've used waxy new potatoes, and haven't overcooked them, this shouldn't be a problem.

Granny's potato salad can be served right after it's mixed, still slightly warm, or chilled and served later, or even the next day when some say it tastes even better.

Potato salad was served on many occasions in Granny's day, and even for Thanksgiving dinner in many homes. But it may have been most delicious when it was part of a summer buffet of cold fried chicken, country ham, biscuits with honey, and sliced red-rich tomatoes.

2 lbs. large new potatoes, peeled and cut into bite-size pieces
¼ cup cider vinegar
1 cup chopped celery (3 or 4 ribs)
1 medium-size onion, chopped (½ cup) or ½ cup thinly sliced green onion
¼ cup chopped parsley
1½ teaspoons salt
¼ teaspoon pepper
1 to 1½ cups mayonnaise, exactly how much depending on how creamy you like your potato salad

Cook potato pieces in lightly salted, boiling water just until tender. Drain thoroughly and turn into a large bowl. Immediately drizzle vinegar over hot potatoes and toss gently. Allow to cool slightly. Add celery, onion, parsley, salt, and pepper and toss gently until thoroughly combined. Add mayonnaise to taste and toss again until well blended. (The potatoes will absorb the mayonnaise as they cool, so you may want to add a bit more later.)

Turn potato salad into a large serving bowl and serve immediately while the salad is still warm, or cover and chill to serve later, or even the next day. Some cooks like to serve potato salad garnished with hard-cooked eggs cut into slices or wedges.

MAKES 4 SERVINGS.

Heart-preserver tips: Reduce the total amount of mayonnaise used and substitute with all or part reduced-fat mayonnaise. Plain yogurt may be used for part of the mayonnaise.

Creamy-Crunchy Coleslaw

Shredding cabbage by Granny's old method is a tedious procedure, for she used a four-sided grater and it took forever. Then she soaked the cabbage in ice water to crisp it, and, of course, it had to be drained almost completely dry before it could be dressed. So, as much as I love coleslaw, I rarely bothered. Just recently, though, thanks to Anne Bailey, a talented, time-saving cook if there ever was one, I started using a long, sharp chef's knife to shred the cabbage and didn't bother to soak it. You can also use the slicing blade (*not* the shredder) of a food processor. The result? We have Granny's Creamy-Crunchy Coleslaw at the drop of my husband's fish hook. (He likes this slaw with fresh-caught, fried flounder.)

1 head cabbage (I prefer the wrinkly Savoy cabbage, but regular green cabbage will do) weighing 1½ to 2 lbs.
1 small onion, shredded on the large holes of a four-sided grater (¼ cup)
¾ cup mayonnaise
2 tablespoons sugar
1 tablespoon fresh lemon juice
⅛ teaspoon salt
⅛ teaspoon pepper
1 tablespoon half-and-half or milk
Paprika for garnish

Remove any wilted outer leaves from the cabbage.

To make cabbage shreds, cut cabbage head in quarters through the core. Cut the core out of each quarter with a small paring knife. Place each cabbage quarter, cut side down, on a cutting surface. Starting at the core end, cut the cabbage into very thin slices with a long, sharp knife, at which point the cabbage will fall into shreds. Place shreds in a large bowl and fluff with your fingers. (I know this will look like a lot of cabbage, but remember that it will wilt down after it is dressed.) Chill cabbage until ready to mix the slaw.

Several hours before serving, or even the day before, add onion to the shredded cabbage and toss to distribute evenly. A big salad serving fork works well for this. In a small bowl, mix mayonnaise, sugar, lemon juice, salt, and pepper. Taste the dressing and adjust seasonings. (Only you know how sweet, salty, or tart you like your coleslaw). Stir in half-and-half.

Gradually stir dressing into cabbage mixture, tossing and turning to thoroughly coat each shred of cabbage. Cover tightly and chill for at least an hour, or until ready to serve.

Turn slaw into a serving bowl and sprinkle with paprika.

MAKES 4 TO 5 CUPS.

Note: This slaw keeps very well for several days. Just remember to take out only what you plan to serve and keep the remainder tightly covered and chilled.

Heart-preserver tip: Substitute reduced-fat mayonnaise for regular mayonnaise. Plain yogurt may also be substituted for part of the mayonnaise.

Easy Apple-y Applesauce

Don't let anyone kid you. *All* applesauce is easy to make. Granny, of course, served two kinds: the one that she made in the autumn from apples straight off the tree in the backyard, and the other from the hundred or so jars that she'd put up.

Some recipes for applesauce are pretty specific about the kinds of apples you should use. Granny and I have been successful using just about any apples that happen to be on the counter, and you can even mix several varieties.

7 or 8 apples (about 3 lbs.), peeled, cored, and cut into chunks
1 cinnamon stick, about 3 inches long, broken in half or in thirds
About 1 cup water
¼ to ½ cup sugar
Few drops lemon juice
Ground cinnamon or nutmeg for garnish

Place apples and cinnamon in a 3-quart saucepan. Add water and set over medium-high heat until water comes to a slow boil. Reduce heat, cover, and simmer for about 15 minutes, or until apples are very soft. Discard cinnamon. Add ¼ cup of the sugar, stirring with a wooden spoon and mashing the apples up against the side of the saucepan. Taste and, if necessary, add more sugar, a tablespoon at a time, until the applesauce is sweet enough to suit you. If it is not tart enough, stir in lemon juice to taste. The sauce should be fairly smooth, although homemade applesauce should have a lump here and there. (You can mash it to a smooth puree, if you like, but Granny and I both feel that this takes away a lot of its character.) If the applesauce seems too wet at this point, simmer it, uncovered, to allow some evaporation.

Cool slightly, then turn the applesauce into a serving bowl (Granny liked to use a cut glass bowl) and sprinkle with ground cinnamon or nutmeg. Serve slightly warm (you cannot imagine how comforting this can be) or at room temperature. Chill leftovers, but bring the amount of applesauce to be served up to room temperature before eating it on subsequent occasions.

MAKES 4 TO 5 CUPS, AND THE RECIPE CAN BE DOUBLED.

Heart-preserver tips: Since applesauce is virtually fat free, it's a good heart food. However, you might want to reduce the sugar a bit, or even use a sugar substitute (*after* the applesauce has finished cooking), which works exceptionally well in applesauce.

Warm, Flaky Biscuits with Honey Butter

Granny wouldn't have *thought* of serving dinner without a basket of warm biscuits on the table. Generally there was an assortment of things to spread on the biscuits, too: butter, of course, apple butter, tart jellies, and always honey—and honey butter.

By the way, if you don't own a 2-inch biscuit cutter, or can't find one, or are simply too lazy to worry about cutting the dough into rounds, you can pat the dough into a ½-inch thick, square-ish shape and cut the biscuit dough into 2-inch squares with a knife.

3 tablespoons butter
1 cup all-purpose flour
1½ teaspoons baking powder
½ teaspoon salt
½ cup whipping cream
1 to 2 tablespoons milk

Preheat oven to 425°F.

In a small skillet or pan, melt butter over low heat and set aside.

Combine flour, baking powder, and salt in a medium bowl. Stir in cream with a fork. The mixture will be crumbly. Add milk, drop by drop, until dough just clings together.

Turn dough out onto a lightly floured surface and knead 8 to 10 times. Roll or press dough out with fingertips until a scant ½-inch thick. Cut dough into 2-inch rounds with a biscuit cutter.

Dip tops of biscuits in melted butter and place on an ungreased baking sheet.

Bake for 12 to 15 minutes, or until biscuits are golden. Remove baking sheet from oven and place on a wire rack to cool slightly. Transfer biscuits to a napkin-lined basket.

MAKES ABOUT 1 DOZEN BISCUITS.

Honey Butter

Whip 3 tablespoons honey into 1 stick (8 tablespoons) softened butter until light and fluffy.

Heart-preserver tips: Brush biscuits lightly with vegetable oil and do not dip in melted butter; skip the honey butter, and substitute plain honey or other fat-free spread.

Real Southern Spoon Bread

To qualify as real comfort food, spoon bread should be served in the Southern manner, or so my Granny said. That is, slathered with softened butter or gravy, or both, and eaten with a fork.

3½ cups milk
6 tablespoons butter
1½ cups white cornmeal
1¼ teaspoons salt
4 well-beaten egg yolks
4 egg whites

Preheat oven to 300°F.

Generously butter a 1½- to 2-quart casserole and set aside.

Reserve ½ cup of the milk. Place remaining 3 cups milk and butter in the top of a double boiler over boiling water. Cook until small bubbles form around the edge of the milk and the butter is melted.

Moisten cornmeal with reserved ½ cup milk in a small bowl. Stir into near-simmering milk and butter. Add salt and cook, stirring constantly, until mixture is thick and smooth, about 2 minutes. Stir in egg yolks and continue to cook, stirring, for 1 minute longer. Remove from heat and set aside.

Beat egg whites in a medium-size, grease-free bowl until stiff peaks form when beaters are lifted.

Scrape cornmeal mixture into a large bowl. Fold in beaten egg whites. Turn into prepared casserole.

Bake for 1 hour, or until lightly browned and just starting to pull away from the side of the dish.

Serve spoon bread directly from the oven in the baking dish.

MAKES 6 TO 8 SERVINGS.

Heart-preserver tip: Just a small spoonful—and just a smidgen of gravy or melted butter.

A Patriotic Strawberry Shortcake

Any self-respecting Granny would have been appalled by latter-day, shortcut renditions of this quintessential American dessert, i.e., a cloying spongecake-from-a-cellophane-package-topped-with-sugary-berries version of strawberry shortcake that a frightening number of moderns accept as the real thing.

Granny started her strawberry shortcake with a not-too-sweet, genuine shortcake split in half. Then she crushed a few of her fresh-picked berries with sugar and mixed these into naturally sweet straw-berry halves. Right before she served it, Granny spooned the berry mixture between and on top of the split shortcake and covered both layers with freshly whipped, lightly sweetened cream. Yum!

2 cups all-purpose flour

¼ cup sugar

1 tablespoon baking powder

½ teaspoon salt

4 tablespoons cold butter, cut into small pieces

¾ cup light cream or half-and-half

2 tablespoons melted butter

*3 pints strawberries, rinsed, then hulled (hulling before rinsing
    makes water-logged berries)*

⅓ cup superfine sugar

*2 cups whipping cream, whipped and lightly sweetened with
    confectioners' sugar*

Preheat oven to 450°F.

Butter two 8-inch round cake pans and set aside.

Combine flour, sugar, baking powder, and salt in a large bowl with a wire whisk until well blended. Cut cold butter pieces into flour mixture with a pastry blender or two knives until the mixture resembles coarse meal. Stir in cream just until moistened. Turn out onto a lightly floured surface and knead just until the dough holds together and forms a ball. Divide dough in half and pat each half into a prepared pan. Brush tops with melted butter.

Bake shortcake for about 15 minutes, or until puffed and golden brown. Remove from pans and cool completely on wire racks.

Place about one fourth of the berries in a large bowl and crush with the back of a heavy spoon. Stir in superfine sugar. Cut remaining berries in half (or in quarters if they're large) and stir into the crushed berries.

Just before serving, place one shortcake layer on a serving plate. Prick the top all over with a fork. Top with half the strawberry mixture, then half the whipped cream. Prick the second layer with the fork. Set second layer on top of first and top with remaining strawberries and cream.

Serve immediately. (Strawberry shortcake should be finished at one sitting. Leftovers tend to be a bit mushy—but delicious, nevertheless.)

MAKES 8 SERVINGS

Heart-preserver tips: Omit brushing with melted butter and go light on the whipped cream.

Mile-High Apple Pie

Most apple pies one encounters these days bear little resemblance to the kind Granny used to make. Her flaky-crust creations, bursting with the special goodness of crisp, juicy apples, freshly picked from the gnarled backyard apple tree, had the kind of texture and flavor combinations that could haunt you forever—and probably do.

Because she always had more apples than she knew what to do with, Granny never skimped when it came to filling a pie, and she mounded the apple slices under the crust giving it a kind of mountainous, lumpy appearance that was anything but unappetizing.

Granny used lard for her crust, naturally, and that was what gave all pie crusts of her era that special, flaky quality that would melt in your mouth. I suggest you do the same, but if you like you can use all shortening or butter (see note) and the crust will still be good.

CRUST:

4 cups all-purpose flour
2 teaspoons salt
1⅓ cups lard (see note for substituting butter or shortening)
½ cup plus 3 to 4 tablespoons ice water

Place flour and salt in a large bowl. Stir with a wire whisk until well blended. With a pastry blender or two knives, cut in the lard until the mixture has a coarse, mealy texture.

Stirring lightly with a fork, sprinkle water over the mixture a spoonful at a time until the dough begins to cling together. Gather the dough into a ball, pressing it together with your hands. Wrap in plastic film and refrigerate 1 to 2 hours before rolling. (The dough may be kept refrigerated for up to two days and may be frozen for up to one month. If frozen, defrost in the refrigerator for a day before using.)

FILLING:

3 lbs. McIntosh apples, peeled, cored, and sliced
1 tablespoon lemon juice
1 teaspoon grated lemon peel
¾ cup sugar
⅓ cup all-purpose flour
1 teaspoon ground cinnamon
2 tablespoons butter, cut into small pieces
Milk for glazing crust
Sugar for sprinkling on crust

Preheat oven to 425°F.

In a very large bowl, toss apples with lemon juice and lemon peel. In a medium-size bowl, mix sugar, flour, and cinnamon until thoroughly combined. Add to apple mixture and toss to coat apples completely. Set aside.

Remove pastry from the refrigerator. Divide ball into thirds. Cut away one third to use for the bottom crust. The remaining two thirds will be used for the top crust. Using a glass pie plate or a dark metal pan as a guide, roll out the smaller piece of pastry on a lightly floured surface with a floured rolling pin. The crust should be at least 1 inch larger all around than the inverted pie plate and about ⅛-inch thick. Fold the pastry circle in half. Gently unfold over the pie plate, gently fitting the pastry inside and allowing the excess to hang over the side. Do not trim the pastry just yet.

Fill pie shell with apple mixture, mounding high in the center. Pour over any juices that have accumulated in the bowl. Dot with butter.

Roll out remaining piece of dough as before, making the circle at least 15 inches in diameter. Cut little vents in the crust with the tip of a sharp knife. Fold pastry in half. Place folded pastry over one half of the filled pie shell. Unfold over the filling, pressing the top and bottom pastry together. Trim both overhanging edges with scissors, leaving a ¼-inch overhang. Using the tines of a dinner fork, firmly press edges of dough onto the rim of the pie dish. Brush pastry with milk and sprinkle with sugar.

Place pie directly on the oven rack in the lower third of the oven. Place a piece of foil on the oven floor to catch any drips. Bake for 40 to 50 minutes, or until crust is appetizingly golden. Cool on a wire rack before cutting.

Serve with a scoop of Granny's Best Vanilla Ice Cream (page 39).

MAKES ONE 9-INCH PIE; ABOUT 8 SERVINGS.

Note: If you wish to substitute butter or shortening for lard, you will have to increase these amounts by 3 tablespoons each, since lard has more shortening power than either butter or shortening. Use 1½ cups butter or shortening instead of the amount of lard called for in the crust recipe.

Heart-preserver tips: Have a bite or two of the crust and concentrate on eating the filling. Exchanging the lard for butter or shortening will have very little effect on the amount of saturated fat in the crust, but the amount of cholesterol will be reduced if shortening is used instead of butter or lard.

Granny's Best Homemade Vanilla Ice Cream

If there is anything better in the world than Granny's apple pie, it is Granny's apple pie with a scoop (or two) of her homemade vanilla ice cream on top. Happy was the summer day when Granny would get out the old wooden ice-cream maker and announce that there would be ice cream for dessert. It was hard work to make ice cream in the old days, but there was also never a shortage of willing volunteers to turn the crank, especially for the immediate reward of being able to lick the dasher.

> *1 quart whipping cream*
> *1 vanilla bean, split in half or 1½ teaspoons vanilla extract (see note)*
> *1 cup sugar*
> *⅛ teaspoon salt*

Pour 2 cups of the cream into a medium-size saucepan. Scrape seeds from vanilla bean into cream. Heat cream just until it begins to bubble around the edge and remove from heat. Stir in sugar and salt until sugar is dissolved. Place cream mixture, still in the saucepan, in the refrigerator to chill. When cold, stir in remaining 2 cups cream. If using vanilla extract, stir that in now.

When ready to make ice cream, pour cold cream mixture into the canister of an ice cream maker and freeze according to the manufacturer's directions.

Scrape ice cream into a freezer container with a tight-fitting lid, leaving about ½-inch headspace. Cover and place in the freezer for 3 or 4 hours to ripen.

MAKES ABOUT 1 QUART.

Note: Granny would never have considered using vanilla extract in her vanilla ice cream and neither should you, for it is the miniscule black vanilla seeds that will distinguish your vanilla ice cream as the genuine article.

Heart-preserver tip: Obviously this is not the sort of recipe that lends itself to the reduction of cholesterol and saturated fat. Better to make this ice cream as an occasional treat to be shared with about eight friends, thereby keeping the servings scanty and guaranteeing no leftovers.

The Deadliest Pecan Pie in the South

Grannies who lived in the south often had pecan trees in the yard instead of apple trees. It was the kids' job to pick up the ripe nuts that fell from the tree. Sometimes it was even necessary to climb the tree and shake the branches to "encourage" the tree to give up some of its precious load. But that was only half the job. Shelling generally took place in the evening to the accompaniment of The Lone Ranger, Burns and Allen, The Green Hornet, The Shadow, and a host of other radio shows that are quickly becoming ever-more-vague memories. The rewards for all this work, of course, were Granny's delectable pecan creations, the most notable being this divine pecan pie.

1 9-inch, unbaked pie shell
1 to 1¼ cups pecan halves
4 eggs
1 cup firmly packed, light-brown sugar
1 cup dark corn syrup
3 tablespoons butter, melted
2 tablespoons good brandy or cognac
Lightly sweetened whipped cream or vanilla ice cream

Preheat oven to 300°F.

Scatter pecan halves in the bottom of the pie shell.

Beat eggs, sugar, and syrup together in a medium bowl. Add butter and mix thoroughly. Stir in brandy. Slowly pour over pecans. Let stand until pecans rise to the surface. (The pecans will become beautifully glazed as the pie bakes.)

Bake for about 1 hour and 30 minutes, or until the center is nearly firm.

Cool pie on a wire rack.

Serve while still slightly warm, topped with whipped cream or ice cream.

MAKES ABOUT 8 SERVINGS.

Heart-preserver tips: Reduce the amount of butter called for, or leave it out entirely, and savor every bite of a small serving. No whipped cream or ice cream, either!

Like Lucille's Lemon Meringue Pie

When I was a little girl we drove down to Florida to visit my grandparents in Delray Beach almost ev⸍ ⸍ winter. While we were there we often visited a restaurant where they didn't serve booze and they didn't take reservations, and we always had to wait in a long line outside before we were finally seated. Ordinarily, my father was not one for queueing up, but the food at Lucille's was so exceptional that he never seemed to mind. One of Lucille's specialties was a lemon pie that was covered with about eight inches of meringue. My father loved that pie and years later, when there was no longer any reason to go to Delray Beach, I made lemon meringue pies like Lucille's for him, adding a couple of extra egg whites to achieve the extra-high meringue topping.

A few words of caution before you begin squeezing lemons. Do not make this pie too far in advance of when it is to be eaten or on a very humid day, since the meringue has a tendency to "weep" and will make the crust soggy. As a matter of fact, a lemon meringue pie should be served within a few hours after it is baked, the sooner the better. It does not keep well—which is hardly ever a problem.

6 eggs

1¾ cups sugar

⅓ cup cornstarch

1½ cups water

⅓ cup fresh lemon juice (2 or 3 lemons)

3 tablespoons butter

2 teaspoons grated lemon peel

⅛ teaspoon cream of tartar

Pinch of salt

1 prebaked, 9-inch pie shell

Preheat oven to 400°F.

Separate eggs, placing 4 of the yolks in a small bowl and the 6 whites in a large, grease-free bowl. (Place remaining unbroken egg yolks in a small cup, cover with cold water, and refrigerate for a day or two for use in another recipe.)

Mix 1 cup of the sugar and cornstarch in a heavy, medium-size saucepan. Add water, stirring until smooth. Stir in egg yolks. Place pan over medium heat. Bring to a slow boil, stirring constantly, and boil for 1 minute. Remove from heat. Stir in lemon juice, butter, and lemon peel. Set aside to cool.

Add cream of tartar and salt to egg whites and beat with an electric mixer on medium speed until foamy. Gradually beat in remaining ¾ cup sugar. Continue beating on high speed until stiff peaks form when beaters are lifted.

Spoon cooled lemon filling into the prebaked pie shell, smoothing with the back of a spoon. With a large, clean spoon, smooth about one fourth of the meringue mixture over the filling and onto the edge of the crust to seal and prevent shrinking. Pile on remaining meringue, shaping into high peaks with the back of a spoon.

Bake for 6 to 8 minutes, or until meringue is golden and tips are appetizingly flecked with brown.

Cool pie on a wire rack. Chill the pie if it is not to be eaten within an hour or two, but do not cover it.

MAKES ONE 9-INCH PIE; 6 TO 8 SERVINGS.

Heart-preserver tip: Your heart loves meringue, for the white of an egg contains not a speck of fat. However, it's another story with the yolk-laden filling, so be content with just a sliver. (You might try trading your filling for another's meringue.)

Spicy Bread Pudding Gilded with a Light Custard Sauce

Bread pudding is one of those foods that might never have been if bread had always stayed fresh for as long as it does in these days of state-of-the-art preservatives.

Back when Granny was baking her own bread, or at least buying it from an old-fashioned bakery, bread only kept for a day or two before it staled and that was when Granny's real talent for waste-not, want-not really shined.

This is one of what must be thousands of versions of bread pudding. In essence, they are all pretty much the same: stale bread, milk, eggs, and sugar. The variations undoubtedly had to do with what the cook had in her larder at the moment.

I enjoy bread pudding an hour or so after it comes from the oven, just as it is, still slightly warm. But, on the other hand, if Granny offered me a little light custard sauce, I probably wouldn't turn it down. By the way, in upscale cooking circles this custard is called *creme anglaise*, which can also be served over rice pudding, poached or raw fruit (poached pears or whole strawberries, for instance), or as a base for floating island, trifle, or pound cake.

4 cups milk
½ cup sugar
⅓ cup unsulphured molasses
1 tablespoon butter
1 teaspoon vanilla extract
½ teaspoon ground cinnamon
¼ teaspoon ground ginger
¼ teaspoon ground nutmeg
¼ teaspoon salt
4 eggs
6 cups (about 10 slices firm bread) dry bread cubes (see note)
½ cup golden or dark raisins

CUSTARD SAUCE:

2 eggs

3 tablespoons sugar

1 cup half-and-half

½ teaspoon vanilla extract

Preheat oven to 350°F.

Butter a shallow, 2-quart baking dish (round, oval, square, or rectangular, it doesn't make any difference) and set aside.

Bring milk to a boil in a medium-size saucepan. (Watch carefully; the milk will boil up and over the side of the pan quicker than you can say "big mess.") Remove from heat and stir in sugar, molasses, butter, vanilla, cinnamon, ginger, nutmeg, and salt.

Beat eggs slightly in a large bowl. Gradually pour hot milk over eggs, stirring rapidly so that the eggs don't begin to "scramble."

Sprinkle bread cubes and raisins in the bottom of the prepared baking dish. Pour milk mixture over bread and raisins and let stand for 10 to 15 minutes, then stir.

Place baking dish in a larger baking dish and pour hot water into the larger dish to come up about 1 inch on the side of the smaller dish.

Bake for 45 to 50 minutes, or until a knife inserted in the center comes out clean.

To make custard sauce, combine eggs and sugar in the top of a double boiler. Add half-and-half and stir over simmering water until mixture coats a metal spoon, 10 to 12 minutes. Stir in vanilla. Pour custard into a small serving bowl.

Serve custard warm or chilled. If you want to chill it, set the bowl of warm custard in a pan of ice and water and stir to cool rapidly. Press a piece of plastic film directly on the surface of the custard to keep a skin from forming and refrigerate until ready to serve.

Bread pudding may be served warm or chilled with warm or chilled sauce.

MAKES 6 TO 8 SERVINGS; ABOUT 1¼ CUPS SAUCE.

Note: For really good bread pudding that isn't mushy, the bread should be really dried out. If yours isn't or you have any doubts, spread the cubes out on wax paper to dry for several hours, or spread the cubes on a baking sheet and place in a 200°F oven, stirring occasionally, until the cubes feel dry to the touch.

Heart-preserver tip: As wholesome as this lovely dish may be, the eggs and half-and-half don't bode well for the heart. So, keep the servings small, please, and omit the custard sauce.

Summer Peach Bake

Every summer, when the branches were bending low under the weight of hundreds of ripe peaches on Granny's tree near the back door, we set about to eat as many as we could out of hand, savoring that never-to-be-forgotten aroma and sweet, sticky juice that ran down our chins and through our fingers. Sometimes Granny just sliced the peaches into bowls and added a little thick cream, the perfect snack or ending to a summer meal. Naturally, she had countless recipes for using fresh peaches, and what we didn't eat one way or another went into mason jars, plain or brandied, to be enjoyed all winter.

If you can get your hands on some juicy, just-picked peaches, and if by chance there are a few that don't get eaten as is, you might like to try one of Granny's peachy summer treats.

6 to 8 firm ripe peaches (about 3 lbs.)
2 tablespoons light- or dark-brown sugar
2 tablespoons butter
1 egg
1 cup granulated sugar
1 cup all-purpose flour
1 teaspoon baking powder
¼ teaspoon salt

Preheat oven to 350°F.

Peel peaches, then slice into a well-buttered, 1½-quart baking dish. Sprinkle with brown sugar and dot with butter.

Beat the egg in a medium-size bowl. Sift into it the granulated sugar, flour, baking powder, and salt. Stir only until the mixture is blended. It will be dry and crumbly. Spoon on top of peaches.

Bake for about 35 minutes, or until crumbs are lightly browned and mixture bubbles around the edge.

Serve warm with cream or ice cream—or just plain.

MAKES 6 SERVINGS.

Heart-preserver tip: Serve without cream or ice cream.

A Tall Yellow Layer Cake with Thick Coconut Frosting

This is the cake that sat on Granny's mahogany sideboard, a mute testimonial to her superior baking skills and love of serving delicious food. Devil's food, angel food, chocolate, burnt sugar, and sponge, great cakes all, cannot rival for one mouthful the incomparable yellow layer cake with thick coconut frosting, the Great American Party Cake.

1 cup butter, softened (2 sticks)
2 cups sugar
3 cups cake flour (not self-rising flour)
1 tablespoon baking powder
1/2 teaspoon salt
4 eggs
2 teaspoons vanilla extract
1 cup milk

FROSTING:
1 1/2 cups sugar
1/3 cup water
2 tablespoons light corn syrup
1/8 teaspoon salt
2 egg whites
1/2 cup marshmallow creme
1 teaspoon vanilla extract
1 can (3 1/2 oz.) flaked coconut

Preheat oven to 350°F.

Grease and flour three 8-inch round cake pans and set aside.

Cream butter in a large bowl. Gradually add sugar, beating until mixture is light and fluffy. (Beat 10 minutes with an electric mixer, longer if beating by hand.)

In another large bowl, mix flour, baking powder, and salt together with a wire whisk until fluffy and set aside.

Add eggs, one at a time, to butter mixture, beating well after each addition. Stir vanilla into milk and add to butter mixture alternately with flour mixture, beginning and ending with flour. Divide batter evenly between prepared cake pans.

Bake for 35 to 40 minutes, staggering cake pans on oven racks, until a wooden pick inserted in the center of the layers comes out clean. Cool cake in pans on wire racks for 10 minutes. Turn out onto racks to finish cooling.

To make frosting, combine sugar, water, corn syrup, salt, and egg whites in the top of a double boiler. Set over boiling water. Beat on high speed with an electric mixer for 5 to 7 minutes, or until mixture forms soft peaks when beaters are lifted. Remove from heat and beat in marshmallow creme and vanilla.

Frost each of two of the cake layers with ⅓ cup frosting, setting one layer on top of another as you do so. Set third layer in place. Use remaining frosting to frost top and side of cake. Press coconut over top and onto side of cake.

MAKES ONE 8-INCH, THREE-LAYER CAKE; 8 TO 12 SERVINGS.

Heart-preserver tip: A very thin slice, as you might have expected, but enjoy the frosting because it contains *no* fat!

Special-Occasion Chocolate Cake

Birthday, Father's Day, graduation from kindergarten, first robin sighted, or whenever the occasion called for something special, Granny was likely to produce this handsome chocolate cake with a delicate, chocolate-buttercream frosting.

2½ cups sifted all-purpose flour
2 teaspoons baking soda
½ teaspoon salt
1 cup milk
1 tablespoon white vinegar
2 cups sugar
1 cup butter-flavor or solid white vegetable shortening
½ cup unsweetened cocoa powder
2 eggs
½ cup hot water
1 teaspoon vanilla extract

FROSTING:
3 squares unsweetened chocolate
½ cup butter, softened (1 stick)
1 box (16 oz.) confectioners' sugar
3 tablespoons milk
2 egg yolks
1 teaspoon vanilla extract

Preheat oven to 350°F.

Grease and flour three, 8-inch round cake pans and set aside.

Sift flour, baking soda, and salt onto a piece of wax paper and set aside.

Combine milk and vinegar in a cup and set aside. Mixture will curdle as it sours.

Beat sugar and shortening together in a large bowl with an electric mixer until light and fluffy. Beat in cocoa, then eggs. Add dry ingredients alternately with soured milk. Stir in hot water and vanilla until well blended. Divide batter evenly between prepared pans.

Bake for 40 minutes, or until the tops of the layers spring back when lightly touched.

Cool cake in pans for 10 minutes on wire racks. Turn out onto racks to cool completely.

To make frosting, melt chocolate in a small, heavy saucepan over hot water. Set aside to cool.

In a medium-size bowl, cream butter. Beat in sugar, milk, egg yolks, and vanilla with an electric mixer until smooth. Stir in cooled chocolate and blend thoroughly. If necessary, add more milk, drop by drop, to give frosting a good spreading consistency.

Level cake layers with a long, serrated knife. Place one layer on a cake plate. Spread with ½ cup frosting. Repeat with remaining layers. Frost side of cake, then spread remaining frosting on top, swirling the frosting to give it a thick, luscious appearance.

MAKES ONE, 8-INCH, THREE-LAYER CAKE; 8 TO 12 SERVINGS.

Heart-preserver tip: A very thin slice, please. There are no redeeming virtues to this cake.

Grandmother Tilghman's Pound Cake

This really is my grandmother's recipe for pound cake. She got it from her mother, who got it from her mother, and so on. It is typical of old-time pound cakes: rich, heavy, and not too sweet, which certainly makes it a lot different from the ready-made pound cakes you might be used to from the supermarket shelf and freezer.

Grandmother almost always had a pound cake on hand in the cool room for impromptu desserts and snacks. This is one of my mother's favorite comfort foods, and she remembers it being served for Sunday-night suppers, cut into layers and spread with jelly, then sprinkled with confectioners' sugar. Other times it was served with custard sauce (see page 44).

Real pound cakes actually do contain a pound each of butter, sugar, flour, and eggs, which makes two loaf cakes. If you want, you can cut the recipe in half and have a half-pound cake.

1 lb. unsalted butter, softened
1 lb. sugar (about 2⅓ cups)
1 lb. eggs (8 to 10 large eggs)
1 tablespoon plus 1 teaspoon vanilla extract
1 teaspoon salt
1 lb. all-purpose flour (about 4 cups)

Before you begin to make this cake, there are a few things Granny would want you to take into consideration to assure success.

If you have a kitchen scale, it would be a good idea to weigh the flour, sugar, and eggs (out of the shell). Weighing the flour is probably the most important since this can change rather dramatically, depending on the brand, the humidity on the day the cake is baked, etc.

Beating the batter well is also important. If enough air is not incorporated into the batter, the finished cake will be too dense and wet. If you are beating by hand, beat the batter hard for at least 3 minutes after the addition of each egg. Some Grannies would say that 5 minutes is not too long. Using an electric hand mixer will reduce the beating time some, but you will probably have to turn it off to cool every now and then. Obviously, a standing mixer is the best appliance for the job, and beating time will be reduced to about 1 minute between the addition of each egg.

Preheat oven to 350°F.

Butter and flour two 9 x 5 x 3-inch loaf pans and set aside.

Cream butter and sugar in the large bowl of an electric mixer, or with a wooden spoon, until the mixture is light and fluffy. Beat in eggs, one at a time, beating thoroughly after each addition (see above). Beat in vanilla extract and salt. Add flour, 1 cup at a time, beating well after each addition, until the flour is completely incorporated and the batter is smooth.

Divide batter evenly between prepared loaf pans, smoothing the tops with a spatula.

Bake in the center of the oven for about 1 hour, or until the cakes are browned on top and just beginning to shrink from the sides of the pans. The cakes will be cracked on top, the trademark of a pound cake, so don't worry about it.

Cool cakes on wire racks in pans for about 5 minutes, then turn out onto racks to cool completely.

MAKES TWO LOAF CAKES; 18 HALF-INCH SERVINGS EACH.

Note: Like all butter cakes, this one keeps well for several days. When cakes have cooled completely, wrap tightly in foil or plastic film and refrigerate. Pound cake may also be frozen. Defrost at room temperature for 1 to 2 hours, letting the cake thaw completely before it is unwrapped.

Granny's Tender Jelly Roll

I'd like to bet that the only jelly roll most of us moderns have ever tasted is the one from the cellophane package on the baked goods' shelf at the supermarket. If that's the case, you can't imagine the delights in store if you'll take the time to make a Granny version of this old favorite. This is the cake, you know, that is baked in a big flat pan with low sides and is then rolled in a kitchen towel to give it its shape.

¾ cup all-purpose flour
1 teaspoon baking powder
½ teaspoon salt
4 eggs, at room temperature
¾ cup sugar
1 teaspoon vanilla extract
½ cup confectioners' sugar
½ cup raspberry jam

Preheat oven to 400°F.

Grease a 15½ x 10½-inch jelly-roll pan and line it with wax paper. Grease and flour the wax paper and set aside.

Combine flour, baking powder, and salt in a large bowl. In another large bowl, beat eggs with an electric mixer until thick and pale colored. Beat in sugar until thick. Beat in vanilla until well blended.

Fold flour mixture into egg mixture. Turn batter into prepared pan, smoothing evenly with a wide spatula.

Bake for about 8 minutes, or until the cake springs back when touched lightly.

While the cake bakes, lay a clean kitchen towel out on a work surface. Place the confectioners' sugar in a small strainer and shake the sugar over the towel to coat it generously. Carefully turn out the hot cake onto the sugared towel. While the cake is still hot, carefully pull off the wax paper. Immediately trim ½ inch from the cake edges with a sharp knife. Gently roll up the warm cake in the towel from a long side. (So it shouldn't surprise or confuse you, the towel will be wrapped up *in* the cake at this point.) Let the cake cool in the towel on a wire rack. When cool, unroll cake and spread with jam. Reroll the cake without the towel and place seam-side down on a serving platter.

Slices of jelly roll may be served plain, with sweetened whipped cream, ice cream, chocolate sauce (page 188), or a light custard sauce (page 44), for instance.

This is old-fashioned baking and eating at its very best.

MAKES ABOUT 8 SERVINGS.

Heart-preserver tip: Serve yourself a half-inch slice and skip any rich enhancements.

Applesauce Cake with Caramel Cream Sauce

A moist, comforting cake that's actually more like a quick bread. It usually sat on Granny's kitchen counter and it was baked more for snacking than for dessert. The sauce is my innovation, a somewhat sinful addition that tastes particularly good when I'm feeling glum.

2 cups (about 8 oz.) walnuts or pecans
2½ cups plus 2 tablespoons all-purpose flour
1 tablespoon ground cinnamon
1 teaspoon ground nutmeg
¼ teaspoon salt
2 cups (from a 22-oz. jar) smooth applesauce
2 teaspoons baking soda
¾ cup butter, softened (1½ sticks)
2 cups sugar

Preheat oven to 350°F.

Grease and lightly flour a 9 x 13-inch baking pan and set aside.

Finely chop nuts, then toss with 2 tablespoons of the flour on a piece of wax paper and set aside.

Thoroughly mix remaining 2½ cups flour with cinnamon, nutmeg, and salt in a medium-size bowl and set aside.

Heat applesauce in a small saucepan over medium heat until hot.

Stir in baking soda (at this point the applesauce will bubble up and turn brown, but don't worry about it) and set aside.

Cream butter and sugar in a large bowl until thoroughly combined. Beat in warm applesauce mixture. Gradually add flour mixture, mixing just until well blended. Stir in nuts until well distributed in the batter.

Turn batter into prepared pan. Bake for 40 minutes, or until the cake begins to pull away from the sides of the pan. Cool cake in pan on a wire rack. Cut cake into squares.

MAKES 12 TO 16 SERVINGS.

Caramel Cream Sauce

To make sauce, combine 1 cup of whipping cream and 2 tablespoons of dark-brown sugar in a large bowl. Let stand 10 minutes to dissolve sugar. Beat with an electric mixer at high speed until soft peaks form when beaters are lifted. Chill until ready to serve.

Heart-preserver tips: As comfort foods go, this one isn't so bad for you; substitute margarine for butter, if you like, and leave the sauce at the other end of the table.

Gingerbread with Hot Lemon Sauce

A recipe for gingerbread that traveled the Oregon Trail with the Great-Great-Great-Granny of a friend. The original version, I'm told, called for bacon fat, which one of the subsequent Grannies changed first to lard and then to butter. The black pepper, which may come as a bit of a surprise in the list of ingredients, is the spice that gives truly old-fashioned gingerbread its familiar "bite." Leave it out if you're the cautious type. The lemon sauce was my own Granny's touch and should be served quite hot. By the way, even if you should decide to cheat and make your gingerbread from a mix, if you take the time to make the sauce, you will hardly know that the cake is not from scratch.

1½ cups all-purpose flour
1 teaspoon baking soda
6 tablespoons butter, softened
½ cup firmly packed light-brown sugar
1 teaspoon ground ginger
1 teaspoon ground cinammon
1 teaspoon ground cloves
¼ teaspoon black pepper
¼ teaspoon salt
½ cup unsulphured molasses
2 eggs
¾ cup sour cream

HOT LEMON SAUCE:
1 small lemon
½ cup sugar
2 tablespoons cornstarch
¼ teaspoon salt
1 cup water
2 tablespoons fresh lemon juice
1 teaspoon grated lemon peel
1 tablespoon butter, softened

Preheat oven to 350°F.

Butter a 9-inch-square baking pan and set aside.

Mix flour and soda thoroughly in a medium bowl and set aside.

Cream butter, brown sugar, ginger, cinnamon, cloves, pepper and salt in a large bowl until fluffy. Blend in molasses. Add eggs, one at a time, beating well after each addition. Add sour cream alternately with reserved flour mixture and beat hard until smooth. Turn into prepared pan.

Bake in the center of the oven for about 30 minutes, or until a wooden pick inserted near the center comes out clean. Cool cake on a wire rack. Cut cake into squares and serve with *hot* lemon sauce.

To make sauce, carefully cut away the lemon peel and the bitter white pith just beneath. Holding the lemon over a bowl, cut between segments with a small, sharp knife, allowing them to fall into the bowl. Set aside.

Combine sugar, cornstarch, and salt in a small saucepan. Stir in water. Cook over low heat, stirring constantly, until mixture thickens and clears. Stir in reserved lemon segments, juice, lemon peel, and butter until well mixed.

MAKES 6 SERVINGS.

Heart-preserver tip: Omit butter from the sauce.

Chocolate-Chunk Cookies

It amuses me to watch my fellow New Yorkers running from one cutesy cookie bakery to another trying to find the chocolate chip cookies they remember so well as a child.

This recipe has all the buttery, brown-sugary goodness of the cookies Granny used to bake. They are easy to make and must surely be cheaper than the ones in the expensive bakeries. But, instead of using chocolate chips, we've substituted BIG chocolate chunks that will still be warm and melting in the cookies if you eat them soon after they're pulled from the oven. A few words about the chocolate. Select a high-quality semisweet chocolate that is meant for eating as well as baking. My choices would be Ghirardelli, Lindt, or Maillard, not necessarily in that order.

12 oz. semisweet chocolate
1½ cups all-purpose flour
¾ teaspoon baking soda
¾ teaspoon salt
⅔ cup butter, softened
½ cup granulated sugar
½ cup firmly packed light-brown sugar
1 tablespoon milk
1 teaspoon vanilla extract
2 eggs, lightly beaten
⅔ cup chopped pecans or walnuts (optional)

Place chocolate in the refrigerator to chill while making cookie batter.

Preheat oven to 375°F.

Mix flour, baking powder, and salt in a medium-size bowl with a wire whisk until light and thoroughly combined. (Using a wire whisk to blend the dry ingredients makes sifting unnecessary in this case.) Set aside.

Combine butter, granulated sugar, brown sugar, milk, vanilla, and eggs in a large bowl. Cream the mixture with a large wooden spoon or an electric mixer. It will appear to be curdled, but not to worry. Gradually add flour mixture, beating well after each addition.

Remove chocolate from the refrigerator. Place on a cutting surface and chop into ¼-inch pieces with a long, sharp knife. Immediately stir chocolate chunks and nuts (if using) into cookie batter.

Drop cookie batter by the measuring tablespoonful onto ungreased cookie sheets, leaving about 2 inches between each cookie.

Bake for 9 to 11 minutes, or until cookies are golden.

Remove cookie sheets from oven and eat some of the cookies right away. Cool the remainder on wire racks, then store in a tightly covered container.

MAKES ABOUT 40 COOKIES

Heart-preserver tip: Eat just *one*!

Big, Soft Molasses Cookies

Granny was always muttering things about "spoiling your appetite," but that never stopped her from dispensing little treats in the kitchen as she worked. How many of us remember sitting at her kitchen table staring down at the worn spot in the linoleum while we drank our milk or lemonade and nibbled on Granny's freshly baked cookies.

These soft molasses cookies were a favorite for many, including my father, whose great-grandmother used to bake a few extra-big cookies just for him.

½ cup butter, softened (1 stick)
½ cup solid white vegetable shortening
1½ cups sugar
½ cup unsulphured molasses
2 eggs, lightly beaten
4 cups all-purpose flour
2¼ teaspoons baking soda
2¼ teaspoons ground ginger
1½ teaspoons ground cloves
1½ teaspoons ground cinnamon
½ teaspoon salt
Granulated sugar for coating cookies

Preheat oven to 350°F.

Cream butter, shortening (Granny would have used lard, of course), and sugar together in a large bowl with a wooden spoon until light and fluffy. Beat in molasses and eggs until thoroughly combined. Set aside.

In another large bowl, mix flour, baking soda, ginger, cloves, cinnamon, and salt with a wire whisk until light and thoroughly combined. (Using a wire whisk to blend the dry ingredients makes sifting unnecessary in this case.)

Gradually stir the flour mixture into the butter mixture until smooth and well blended.

Roll pieces of dough into 1½-inch balls between palms of hands. Roll the balls in sugar and place them about 2½ inches apart on ungreased baking sheets.

Bake for 13 minutes. Cookies will flatten as they bake.

Remove cookies from oven and immediately transfer to wire racks to cool. Store in a tightly covered container to keep them from drying out.

MAKES ABOUT 40 COOKIES.

Heart-preserver tip: Eat just *one!*

Granny's Very Special Sugar Cookies

It goes without saying that Granny was a masterful cookie baker. She could produce dozens of varieties without so much as a peek at the ring binder where she kept certain "receipts" and food notes. Our fondest mental image is of her removing a baking sheet laden with fragrant cookies from the oven.

These truly old-fashioned sugar cookies were probably the most popular in her repertoire. They are the cookies that took on magical images and gay colors for most holidays, especially Christmas, when Granny would invite us to help. It was then that many of us got our first cooking lessons when Granny brought out the big, heavy rolling pin and battered cookie cutters and encouraged us to express ourselves. The kitchen was a wreck when the cookies were finally baked and cooling on "tea towels" spread out on the big dining room table, and we were proud and happy, though half sick from eating raw dough.

2 cups sugar

1 cup butter, softened (2 sticks)

4 eggs, well beaten

2 to 4 tablespoons milk

2 teaspoons vanilla extract

5 cups all-purpose flour

4 teaspoons baking powder

½ teaspoon salt

Cream sugar and butter in a large bowl until light and fluffy. (An electric mixer works best for this job, but you can use a big wooden spoon and a lot of elbow grease.) Beat in eggs, 2 tablespoons of the milk, and vanilla until smooth.

Mix flour, baking powder, and salt in another large bowl with a wire whisk until light and thoroughly combined. (Using a wire whisk to blend the dry ingredients makes sifting unnecessary in this case.)

Gradually beat flour mixture into butter mixture. If the mixture seems dry, add another tablespoon or two of milk. Gather dough up into a ball and divide into eight parts. Wrap each part in plastic film or foil. At this point you should refrigerate the dough for several hours or overnight before you attempt to roll it. If you like, you can even freeze the packages of dough until you are ready to bake the cookies.

When ready to bake, remove dough from the refrigerator a package at a time. (Transfer frozen dough to the refrigerator several hours or overnight before baking.)

Preheat oven to 350°F.

Roll one package of dough at a time to about a ⅛-inch thickness on a generously floured surface. It helps to flour the rolling pin, too. This dough tends to be a bit sticky.

Cut dough into shapes with cookie cutters, transferring them to lightly greased baking sheets. Reroll and cut scraps. Decorate cookies on the sheets with colored sugar, nuts, candied fruits, or whatever suits your fancy. Bake for 10 to 12 minutes, or until lightly browned.

With a spatula, nudge the cookies onto a kitchen-towel-covered surface to cool completely. When cool, store in a tightly covered container. These cookies keep well for a week or two.

MAKES ABOUT 8 DOZEN BIG, LITTLE, AND MEDIUM-SIZE COOKIES.

Heart-preserver tip: Eat one big, three little, or two medium-size cookies per day during Christmas week.

Chewy Oatmeal Cookies

Hot oatmeal, with lots of sugar and butter, has always been one of my special comfort foods. If you are similarly inclined, you will undoubtedly enjoy my grandmother's special kind of oatmeal cookies, which are more like a macaroon than a cookie.

Because Grandmother rarely recorded any of her recipes, most of the things she made were lost forever, including these chewy oatmeal cookies—or so I thought. But diligence has its rewards, and not long ago I discovered a recipe in a turn-of-the-century cookbook that looked suspiciously like the one I remember her putting together on the enamel table in her kitchen. You can imagine the thrill when, after a few tests and minor alterations, I duplicated exactly those wonderful oatmeal cookies. Don't think I've left the flour out of the list of ingredients. These cookies have none and that's why they're so sweet and chewy and oatmealy.

4 tablespoons butter, softened
¾ cup firmly packed light-brown sugar
¼ cup granulated sugar
2 eggs
1 teaspoon vanilla extract
2½ cups old-fashioned rolled oats
1 teaspoon baking powder
¼ teaspoon salt

Grease one or two baking sheets and set aside.

Beat butter, brown sugar, and granulated sugar in a medium-size bowl with an electric mixer on low speed until combined. Beat in eggs and vanilla until thick and light.

In another medium-size bowl, mix oats, baking powder, and salt. Gradually stir into butter mixture, mixing thoroughly. Most important: Refrigerate batter for 1 hour.

Preheat oven to 375°F.

Drop batter by measuring tablespoonfuls onto prepared baking sheets.

Bake for 8 minutes, or until edges are browned. Cool on baking sheets for about 5 minutes. Remove to a wire rack to cool completely.

MAKES 36 TO 40 COOKIES.

Heart-preserver tip: Enjoy with reasonable abandon.

A Nice Comfortable Coffee Cake

No one ever left Granny's house without being fed. If there was nothing very exciting in the pantry, like a cake or a pie left over from dinner the night before, this is the sort of coffee cake Granny might have put together early in the morning to offer neighbors, a handyman, or anyone else (including us!) who came through the back door. Granny would serve her coffee cake in big squares accompanied by steaming cups of her impeccably brewed coffee.

STREUSEL TOPPING:

1/3 cup firmly packed light-brown sugar
2 tablespoons all-purpose flour
1/2 teaspoon ground cinnamon
2 tablespoons butter
1/4 cup chopped pecans

CAKE:

1 1/2 cups all-purpose flour
1/2 cup sugar
2 teaspoons baking powder
1/4 teaspoon salt
1/2 cup milk
4 tablespoons butter, melted
1 egg

Preheat oven to 375°F.

Grease an 8-inch-square baking pan and set aside.

To make topping, stir brown sugar, flour, and cinnamon together in a small bowl. Cut butter into sugar mixture with a pastry blender or two knives until mixture resembles coarse crumbs. Stir in nuts and set aside.

To make cake, mix flour, sugar, baking powder, and salt in a medium-size bowl with a wire whisk until light and thoroughly combined. (Using a wire whisk to blend the dry ingredients makes sifting unnecessary in this case.)

Combine milk, melted butter, and egg in a small bowl. Add to dry ingredients and stir just until moistened.

Spoon batter into prepared pan. Sprinkle with streusel topping.

Bake for 25 minutes, or until a wooden pick inserted in the center comes out clean.

Let stand for about 15 minutes before cutting and serving.

MAKES 8 SERVINGS.

Heart-preserver tip: This coffee cake is not terribly high in fat. Go ahead and guiltlessly enjoy a piece.

Fresh-Lemon Lemonade

Granny only knew how to make lemonade one way: with fresh lemons, sugar, and water. (Lemons, by the way, were a rather precious commodity in her day, so a pitcher of lemonade was a real treat.) Granny would probably be fascinated and amused by all the convenience products we have today to turn out a simple pitcher of lemonade (and she probably would have laughed herself silly if she knew about instant iced tea!). But she probably would not have been surprised, or amused, to find out that none of them really taste and smell like an icy glass of the real thing.

Treat yourself to a glass of this lemonade on a hot day. Close your eyes as you sip and you may be able to hear the squeak of the swing on Granny's front porch.

8 cups water
2 cups sugar
12 to 16 lemons
1 lemon, thinly sliced
Mint sprigs for garnish

Place 2 cups of the water and then sugar in a medium-size saucepan. Set over medium-high heat and bring to a simmer, stirring until sugar is dissolved. Remove from heat and set aside.

Squeeze enough lemons to make 2 cups of juice, removing seeds and connective fiber before measuring, but leaving the pulp in the juice. (If you'd rather have a clear lemonade, strain the juice and then measure it.)

Stir sugar-water mixture, lemon juice, and remaining 6 cups water together in a large pitcher. Cover and chill.

Just before serving, stir lemon slices into lemonade. Pour over ice cubes in tall glasses and garnish with mint sprigs.

MAKES ABOUT 11 REFRESHING CUPS.

II

NURSERY FOOD

(Or, I'd Really Rather Be

Sucking My Thumb)

Actually, the best thing about being a little kid is that the older we get the better that short period of our lives becomes. Childhood had its jagged edges, too, but aging tends to smooth them.

For the really bad times (death, a cheating lover, or turning thirty, forty, fifty, sixty, or seventy—after seventy we're supposedly grateful to have gotten that far, or so I'm told) only certain insipid, "white" foods, preferably eaten in solitude, can make us feel better and face the tomorrow with at least limited optimism.

Real Hot Cocoa

Many of us have been opening little packets of cocoa mix for so long that we've forgotten what *real*, honest-to-God cocoa tastes like. Others of us have never tasted this soothing drink. You might not want to bother with this on a busy work morning, but hot cocoa, along with a piece of buttered toast, certainly can perk up a grim Sunday night.

> *2 tablespoons unsweetened cocoa powder*
> *3 tablespoons sugar, or to taste*
> *¼ cup hot water*
> *1½ cups milk*
> *Regular-size marshmallows*

Mix cocoa and sugar in a small saucepan. Gradually stir in hot water. Place pan over medium heat and bring to a boil. Lower heat and cook for 2 minutes, stirring constantly. Stir in milk. Cook until the mixture is as hot as you can get it *without boiling*.

Remove from heat and beat with a rotary beater until foamy. (This step intensifies the flavor of the chocolate and prevents a skin from forming on top as the cocoa begins to cool.)

Top with a marshmallow—or two.

MAKES 2 GENEROUS CUPS.

Heart-preserver tip: It won't be as rich and delicious, of course, but you can substitute skim milk for whole milk.

Creamy Rice Pudding

This is an excellent recipe that produces a creamy rice pudding without all the bother of baking it in the oven. By the way, the secret to a creamy rice pudding is *not* to use converted rice, which, because of the way it's processed, never gets really soft and creamy.

1 quart half-and-half
½ cup regular long-grain rice
½ cup sugar
¼ teaspoon salt
1 teaspoon vanilla extract
½ cup raisins (optional)
Ground cinnamon or nutmeg

In the top of a double boiler, stir together half-and-half, rice, sugar, and salt. Cover and cook over simmering water for 2 hours, stirring frequently to separate the rice grains, or until rice is tender and mixture is creamy. (Don't forget to add hot water to the bottom of the boiler, from time to time.) Stir in vanilla. If using raisins, stir into pudding after cooking. Eat right away, or cover and chill. (It will thicken some when chilled.)

Eat rice pudding chilled, bring to room temperature before serving, or warm in the microwave oven, whichever way you remember. Sprinkle pudding with ground cinnamon or nutmeg before digging in.

MAKES 4 CUPS

Heart-preserver tip: You can substitute whole milk for the half-and-half, of course, but then the pudding will not be nearly as creamy and that creaminess has a lot to do with what makes it comforting. Better you should opt for one small serving and give the rest away at the office.

Chocolate Pudding

Yes, *of course* you can open up a package of chocolate pudding (or even instant pudding) and make that. But if you've got a few minutes (it's been my experience that during the darker periods of my life I've always had too much time), you might want to make this childhood favorite from scratch.

½ cup sugar
⅓ cup unsweetened cocoa powder
3 tablespoons cornstarch
⅛ teaspoon salt
1½ cups milk
½ cup half-and-half

Stir together sugar, cocoa, cornstarch, and salt with a wire whisk in a heavy, medium-size saucepan, until completely combined. Stir in ¼ cup of the milk until the mixture is smooth. Stir in remaining 1¼ cups milk and half-and-half.

Place saucepan over medium heat and cook, stirring constantly with a wooden spoon, until mixture comes to a boil. Continue to cook, stirring 20 times more. Divide mixture between 4 dessert bowls.

Eat right away, or press a piece of plastic wrap directly on the surface of the pudding to prevent a skin from forming. (If you like to plunge a spoon through the skin, then omit this step.) Chill for several hours.

Serve with a little cream poured onto the surface or a big spoonful of whipped cream.

MAKES 4 SERVINGS.

Heart-preserver tip: Even half a serving should bring instant relief.

Condensed-Milk Caramel Pudding

Up until a few years ago, this pudding was cooked at a very low heat in the unopened can. Most of the time everything turned out okay, but sometimes it didn't. It doesn't take a genius to realize that if an unopened can is heated, no matter how gently, it's an explosion waiting to happen. If by some chance you have a copy of that recipe among your Granny's old "receipts," *throw it away*—or frame it—but don't use it to make caramel pudding, or you may have another big problem to add to your list of woes. Use this recipe. It's safe, it's easy, and it tastes exactly the same.

Preheat oven to 425°F.

Open a 14-oz. can of sweetened condensed milk and pour the contents into a pie plate. Cover the pie plate tightly with foil. Place in a slightly larger pan of hot water.

Bake for 1 hour, or until thick and slightly caramel-colored. Remove foil.

Chill before serving.

MAKES ABOUT 4 SERVINGS.

Heart-preserver tip: It's impossible to eat enough of this cloying pudding to do any real harm. Or you may prefer to use it as a dessert topping.

Nursery-Style French Toast

This should not be confused with the French version of French toast found on page 156. N-S.F.T. is quick to make and is intended for mornings when to do much more than make a pot of coffee would be a character-building experience. It can be made with fresh bread, if that's all you have on hand, but is much better and easier to handle if the bread is stale, or at least dried out a little.

1 egg
3 tablespoons milk
1 teaspoon sugar
⅛ teaspoon salt
Butter
3 slices white or whole-wheat bread

Beat egg with milk, sugar, and salt in a wide, shallow bowl or pie plate. Heat butter in a large skillet. One at a time, and working quickly, dip each bread slice into egg mixture, turning to coat, but do not allow the bread to become soggy. Brown on both sides in bubbly-hot butter.

Serve with syrup, honey, or sugar.

Cold milk is soothing with N-S.F.T.

MAKES 1 TO 3 SERVINGS.

Note: I know you may not be in the mood to think about this now, but when better times come, and they will, you'll find this recipe useful for using up slices of hard rolls or French bread.

Chicken Sandwich

I wish I could remember which millionaire it was who was said to have ordered his staff to have a roast chicken in the refrigerator of every one of his houses at all times, but it would probably be safe to say that whoever he was he knew the value of a *real* chicken sandwich, which should not even be mentioned in the same breath as a chicken-roll sandwich. You don't have to roast a chicken in order to make a chicken sandwich (although it would be nice). All you need to do is poach a chicken breast, chill it, and there you have it. Then, if you're up to it, you can put the skin and breast bones back in the broth and simmer everything, tightly covered, for a little while longer. Remove skin and bones, bayleaf, and peppercorns. Add a handful of rice and boil a little longer. Then you know what you've got? More comfort food.

2 whole chicken breasts, each weighing about 1 lb., split
1 medium onion, coarsely chopped
2 ribs celery, coarsely chopped
2 tablespoons chopped parsley
1 large bay leaf
2 teaspoons salt
½ teaspoon dried thyme
¼ teaspoon peppercorns
White bread or white toast
Mayonnaise
Salt and pepper, to taste
Lettuce leaves (optional)

Place rinsed chicken breasts in a pot just large enough to hold them without crowding. Add onion, celery, parsley, bay leaf, salt, thyme, and peppercorns, and enough water to cover. Cover tightly and bring to a simmer. Simmer gently for 12 minutes. Without uncovering, remove pot from heat. Allow to cool undisturbed, during which time the chicken will finish cooking to a succulent goodness. Remove chicken from broth and drain well. Wrap each breast half tightly in foil or plastic film and chill. (If you want to make soup, pull off the skin and pull the bones out of the breast before wrapping and chilling.)

To make a sandwich, discard skin and thinly cut meat from breast halves into large slices, allowing half a breast for each sandwich. Coat bread with mayonnaise to taste. Place two layers of chicken on half the bread slices. Season with salt and pepper. Cover with one piece of lettuce (if using), then the second slice of bread.

Cut sandwiches in half to serve. Sweet gherkin pickles and a glass of milk taste good with this.

YIELD: 4 SANDWICHES.

Heart-preserver tip: Poached chicken is heart food! Just go light on the mayonnaise, or substitute with reduced-fat mayonnaise.

A Very Thin Grilled Cheese Sandwich

The grilled cheese sandwiches one gets nowadays are simply too thick, and are often served open-faced after being run under the restaurant broiler. Pure laziness, I say. There is only one kind of grilled cheese sandwich: the kind Mommy made for lunch on cold days. It should be nibble-thin and made with American cheese. Serve this thin buttery sandwich with tomato soup, if you're very hungry, and a glass of milk, or a milkshake (see page 138), if you're very thin—or just don't give a hang about the calories.

2 slices American cheese
2 slices white bread
Butter

Sandwich cheese between slices of bread. (You can spread the bread with mustard for a more adult version, if you like.) Heat about a tablespoon of butter in a small skillet. When it is foamy, place the sandwich in the skillet. Place the bottom of a slightly larger skillet directly on the sandwich. If the second skillet is not very heavy, weight it down with something—like a rock or a heavy can. Cook over medium heat until you think the sandwich is appetizingly browned on one side, a minute or so. Remove skillet and turn sandwich over. Replace skillet and cook for another minute or two.

Cut sandwich into triangles to serve.

MAKES 1 SANDWICH.

Heart-preserver tip: Substitute margarine for butter, and use reduced fat American cheese.

Lemon Wafers

This is the sort of wholesome little cookie that nannies, or mommies, used to give to good little children. They are a tiny bit chewy and seem to contain the hallucinogenic ability to bring visions of rocking horses, red balls, and blackboards sharply into focus.

½ cup butter, softened (1 stick)
½ cup sugar
1 egg
½ teaspoon vanilla extract
¾ teaspoon grated lemon peel
1 cup all-purpose flour
1 teaspoon baking powder
¼ teaspoon salt

Preheat oven to 350°F.

Grease two baking sheets and set aside.

Beat butter and sugar in a medium-size bowl until well blended. Beat in egg, vanilla, and lemon peel.

In another medium-size bowl, mix flour, baking powder, and salt with a wire whisk until light and thoroughly combined. (Using a wire whisk to blend the dry ingredients makes sifting unnecessary in this case.)

Gradually add flour mixture to butter mixture, beating until well combined.

Drop batter by rounded measuring teaspoonfuls onto prepared baking sheets.

Bake for 6 to 8 minutes, or until golden and lightly browned around the edges. Remove from cookie sheets to wire racks to cool.

MAKES ABOUT 3 DOZEN.

Heart-preserver tip: Substitute margarine for butter.

Patti's Grandmother's Scones

My boarding-school roommate claimed that just a sniff of her grandmother's scones made her feel better, so you can imagine what acutually *eating* one will do for you.

2⅓ cups cake flour (not self-rising flour)
¼ cup plus 2 tablespoons sugar
2 teaspoons baking powder
½ teaspoon salt
6 tablespoons solid white vegetable shortening
½ cup currants
2 eggs
6 tablespoons whipping cream

Preheat oven to 425°F.

Grease one or two baking sheets and set aside.

Mix flour, ¼ cup of the sugar, baking powder, and salt in a large bowl with a wire whisk until thoroughly blended. Add shortening and cut in with a pastry blender or two knives until the mixture resembles coarse crumbs. Stir in currants. Separate one of the eggs and reserve 1 tablespoon of the white. Beat the rest of the egg with the remaining egg. Add to flour mixture with cream and stir until the mixture is just combined.

With floured hands, pat dough to a thickness of about ½ inch on a lightly floured surface. Cut into 2-inch rounds with a floured biscuit cutter, placing the rounds on a prepared baking sheet as you cut. Reroll scraps and cut out remaining dough. Brush tops of scones with reserved egg white. Sprinkle with remaining 2 tablespoons sugar.

Bake for 12 to 15 minutes, or until tops are lightly browned.

Serve warm with jam, if you like. A hot cup of tea is mandatory. Store leftover scones in a tightly covered container after they have cooled.

MAKES 12 TO 14 SCONES.

Note: As well as reheating nicely, leftover scones are also good toasted. Split and brush with melted butter. Run under the oven broiler until appetizingly browned.

Heart-preserver tip: Substitute milk for cream and eat just one.

Linda Greenhouse's Sweet Carrot Cake

I once saw two loaves of this fabulous breadlike cake disappear in a matter of minutes at an ultra-sophisticated party. The hostess baked the breads and served them as sort of an afterthought to fill out a table that was already groaning with the most lavish, up-to-date delicacies New York has to offer. Sort of tells you something, doesn't it?

1 lb. carrots, shredded (about 5 cups)
2 cups sugar
1 cup butter, cut into pieces (2 sticks)
½ cup water
2½ cups all-purpose flour
1 tablespoon ground cinnamon
2 teaspoons ground cloves
2 teaspoons baking soda
¾ teaspoon ground allspice
¾ teaspoon ground nutmeg
½ teaspoon baking powder
½ teaspoon salt
2 eggs
1 cup golden raisins
Confectioners' sugar

Heavily butter and flour two 8½ x 4½ x 2⅝-inch loaf pans and set aside.

Preheat oven to 350°F.

Combine carrot, sugar, butter, and water in a heavy, 3-quart saucepan. Bring to a boil over medium heat, stirring frequently. Lower heat and simmer for 5 minutes. Set aside to cool. (This will take about 2 hours.)

Mix flour, cinnamon, cloves, baking soda, allspice, nutmeg, baking powder, and salt in a large bowl with a wire whisk until light and thoroughly combined. (Using a wire whisk to blend the dry ingredients makes sifting unnecessary in this case.)

In another large bowl, beat eggs until they are thick and lemon-colored. Add cooled carrot mixture, flour mixture, and raisins, stirring just until the batter is well combined.

Divide batter evenly between prepared pans.

Bake for about 1 hour, or until a wooden pick inserted in the center comes out clean. Cool on a wire rack for 10 minutes, then remove from pan to cool completely. Dust with confectioners' sugar before slicing.

Cake may be frozen whole, or in slices. Tightly wrap cooled loaves or slices in plastic film or foil. Thaw while still wrapped at room temperature.

MAKES 2 LOAVES; ABOUT 8 SERVINGS PER LOAF.

Heart-preserver tip: Substitute margarine for butter.

Bread-and-Butter Pudding

Once, while job hunting in New York (a depressing endeavor, if there ever was one), I stopped for lunch at a busy, unimpressive restaurant in lower Manhattan. I ordered dessert, which turned out to be this pudding, only because it came with the lunch. I wish I could tell you that I found a job that afternoon. I didn't, but the pudding, which I finally managed to re-create after many tries, changed my whole outlook that day and has been doing so, from time to time, ever since.

1 tablespoon butter, softened
6 ½-inch thick slices stale French bread
3 eggs
1 egg yolk

2 cups milk
½ cup whipping cream
½ cup sugar
1 teaspoon vanilla extract
Pinch of ground nutmeg
Pinch of salt

Preheat oven to 375°F.

Butter one side of each slice of bread. Layer slices, buttered-side up, in a small (about 1-quart) baking dish.

Beat together eggs, yolk, milk, cream, sugar, vanilla, nutmeg, and salt in a medium-size bowl just until combined. Pour over bread and set aside for 20 minutes.

Place bread-filled dish in a larger pan. Fill larger pan with enough hot water to come halfway up the side of the baking dish.

Bake for about 35 minutes, or until a knife inserted in the center comes out clean. Immediately remove from pan of hot water and cool on a wire rack.

Serve pudding chilled or slightly warm.

MAKES 4 SERVINGS.

Heart-preserver tip: Substitute margarine for butter, and half-and-half for whipping cream.

Two Kinds of Annie's Muffins

Annie Bailey is an accomplished baker and she loves a tender muffin almost better than anything. Put this incomparible combination together and you've got what may be the world's greatest nursery food, better than any nanny (and maybe any mommy) ever made. I know it's an overused expression, but Annie's muffins really do seem to melt in your mouth.

Annie says these muffins can be frozen or refrigerated and reheated, which makes a warm, homemade muffin a definite possibility any old morning you want one.

Plain Muffins with Streusel Topping

TOPPING:
⅓ cup all-purpose flour
¼ cup sugar
½ teaspoon ground cinnamon
3 tablespoons butter, at room temperature

MUFFINS:
2 cups all-purpose flour
⅓ cup sugar
1 tablespoon baking powder
½ teaspoon salt
1 cup milk
1 egg
1 teaspoon vanilla extract
⅓ cup butter, melted

To make streusel topping, combine flour, sugar, and cinnamon in a small bowl; cut in butter until mixture comes together in large crumbs. Set aside.

Preheat oven to 375°F.

Grease 8 2½-inch muffin-pan cups and set aside.

Combine flour, sugar, baking powder, and salt in a large bowl.

In a small bowl, combine milk, egg, and vanilla. Add egg mixture to flour mixture along with melted butter. Stir just until blended.

Divide batter among prepared muffin cups. Sprinkle muffins with topping mixture, dividing evenly.

Bake for 20 to 25 minutes, or until golden and puffed. Let cool in the pan for 5 minutes. Remove from pan, trying to disturb the topping as little as possible.

Serve warm with softened butter.

MAKES 8 MUFFINS.

Blueberry Muffins

1¾ cups all-purpose flour
2½ teaspoons baking powder
½ teaspoon salt
½ cup sugar
¾ cup milk
1 egg
⅓ cup butter, melted
*1¼ cups fresh or frozen blueberries (thaw frozen berries), lightly
    mashed with a fork*
¼ teaspoon ground cinnamon

Preheat oven to 400°F.

Grease 12 2½-inch muffin-pan cups and set aside.

Combine flour, baking powder, salt and *all but 1 tablespoon of the
sugar* in a large bowl.

Combine milk and egg in a small bowl. Add egg mixture to flour
mixture along with melted butter. Stir just until blended. Stir in
blueberries.

Divide batter between prepared muffin cups. Combine remaining
1 tablespoon sugar and cinnamon in a small bowl and sprinkle over
muffins.

Bake for 16 to 20 minutes, or until a wooden pick inserted in the
center comes out clean.

Cool in muffin pans for 5 minutes before removing.

MAKES 12 MUFFINS

Heart-preserver tip: Eat just one—or two; freeze the rest.

III SATURDAY-NIGHT SPECIALS:
Mom's Most Memorable
Labor-Savers

Back in the so-called carefree days of the thirties, forties, and fifties, Saturdays were about as busy in their own way as they are now. It was traditionally a "semi–day off" for Mom, who would go off with us to buy new school shoes after planning an easy early dinner (we'd eat at five instead of six) so that the family would be ready to gather in front of the television to watch Sid, Imogene, and Jackie. Or, before the days of widespread TV, go off together to the seven o'clock show at "Loewie's" theater.

Saturday-night food was a special kind of good and cozy, the closest thing there was to junk food in those days: food that Mom may have perceived as being less than well balanced, consisting of only three dishes instead of six, but okay for one night of the week. These meals were less formal, too. Saturday-night supper was often served at the big kitchen table, and it was a happy time, because Saturday-night foods were often our favorites. And then there was Sunday and the funny papers to look forward to, no work the next day (Dad often had to labor on Saturday in the carefree days) and, of course, no school and no homework.

If the world's got you down, Saturday-night food can make it better any night of the week.

My Mother's Plain Good Meat Loaf

There are undoubtedly thousands of recipes for meat loaf in the world, and thousands more variations on those thousands. Meat loaf recipes can call for several kinds of ground meat, bound together with every variety of wheat product you can think of. Every family has their own favorite. Faced with this dilemma, I finally settled on my own mother's very typical American meat loaf, mainly a combination of ground beef and corn flakes. It sounds dull, I know, yet every time I eat it I never fail to be surprised at how incredibly good it is.

My mother never bothered with it (Mom is still a bit of a lazy cook), but some moms liked to add a little surprise by sticking a couple of hard-cooked eggs or dill pickles, layed end to end, in the middle of the meat loaf, and you can, too. We were not of the school that smeared the meat loaf with catsup before it was baked, either, but you can do that, too.

Meat loaf at our house was *always* served with stewed tomatoes and macaroni-and-cheese and nothing else, the thick tomatoes taking the place of gravy. You might prefer an accompaniment of mashed potatoes (page 18) and gravy.

1½ lbs. lean ground beef (such as round or sirloin)
1 large onion, finely chopped (1 cup)
1 egg, lightly beaten
⅓ cup catsup
¼ teaspoon salt
¼ teaspoon pepper
1½ cups corn flakes
2 tablespoons dried parsley (you can use ¼ cup chopped
*   fresh parsley, if you like)*
2 tablespoons all-purpose flour, for gravy

Preheat oven to 350°F.

Gently, but thoroughly, mix ground beef and onion in a large bowl with your hands (or a large, wooden, salad-serving fork works well).

Add egg, catsup, salt, and pepper and mix again. Add corn flakes and parsley (if using) and mix again.

Turn meat mixture out onto a work surface and shape it into a firm, oval loaf. Transfer the meat loaf to a rack in a shallow baking pan.

Bake for 1 hour.

Remove from oven and transfer meat loaf to a serving platter. Cover lightly with foil and allow it to rest for 10 or 15 minutes before slicing. (This meat loaf tends to be a little crumbly.)

Skim all but about 2 tablespoons of fat from the roasting pan. Mix flour and about 1 cup water in a small bowl. Pour into the hot drippings and cook over medium heat, stirring with a wire whisk, until well blended. Add another cup of water or so and continue to cook, stirring, for a minute or two. Stir in salt and pepper to taste. (If the gravy looks pale and unappetizing at this point, you can stir in a few drops of liquid browning sauce. Although this little coloring trick isn't very popular these days, all moms used to do it and I still think it's better than serving an anemic-looking gravy.)

MAKES 6 SERVINGS.

Heart-preserver tip: Just a thin slice or two of meat loaf (about 3 oz.) and a small spoonful of gravy, if you must.

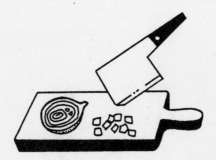

Specially Stewed Tomatoes

Thick and slightly sweetened stewed tomatoes took the place of gravy at our house when my mother served meat loaf. On one side of the plate were a couple of thick slices of meat loaf, and on the other side macaroni-and-cheese, with stewed tomatoes liberally spooned over each. These tomatoes are good over mashed potatoes, too, or almost anytime you'd like a fat-free substitute for gravy.

2 cans (about 16 oz. each) whole tomatoes
1 tablespoon all-purpose flour
1 to 2 teaspoons sugar
½ teaspoon salt
⅛ teaspoon pepper

Drain tomatoes into a saucepan, reserving most of the juice in a small bowl. Cut up tomatoes, right in the saucepan, with the side of a metal spoon.

Gradually add flour to reserved juice, stirring until smooth. Stir into tomatoes. Cook over medium-high heat, stirring constantly, until bubbly and thickened. Add sugar to taste, salt, and pepper.

MAKES 6 SERVINGS.

Heart-preserver tip: Fat free! Indulge!

Creamy Macaroni-and-Cheese

If you like your macaroni-and-cheese the way I do, that is, the macaroni elbows swimming in a creamy cheese sauce with a crusty topping, I guarantee you'll *love* this:

5 tablespoons butter
¼ cup all-purpose flour
2½ cups milk, scalded
¼ teaspoon Worcestershire sauce
⅛ teaspoon ground red pepper
1 package (8 oz.) pasteurized process cheese spread loaf
  (Velveeta!)
1 package (8 oz.) elbow macaroni, cooked as package directs for
  macaroni that will be cooked further, and drained thoroughly
⅓ cup dry, unflavored breadcrumbs

Preheat oven to 375°F.

Lightly grease a 1½- to 2-quart casserole and set aside.

Melt 3 tablespoons of the butter in a large saucepan over medium heat. Stir in flour until smooth. Using a wire whisk, stir in milk all at once and continue cooking until mixture comes to a boil, stirring constantly. Cook, stirring, for 1 minute longer. Remove from heat and stir in Worcestershire sauce and red pepper. Stir in cheese until melted. Stir in cooked, drained macaroni. Spoon into prepared casserole.

In a small saucepan, melt remaining 2 tablespoons butter. Remove from heat and stir in bread crumbs. Sprinkle crumbs over macaroni mixture in casserole.

Bake for 25 to 30 minutes, or until sauce is bubbly and crumbs are appetizingly browned.

MAKES ABOUT 6 SIDE-DISH SERVINGS, OR 3 TO 4 MAIN-DISH SERVINGS.

Heart-preserver tips: Substitute margarine for butter, and skim milk for whole milk when making sauce. Reduce or omit butter in topping crumbs.

Franks and Baked, Baked Beans

For some of us it's enough to heat a can of baked beans and boil some hot dogs. In that case, read no further. However, if you think you might prefer a pot of slow-cooked beans with chunks of frankfurters cooked right in it, try this. Another Saturday night you can try substituting chunks of kielbasa (Polish sausage) for the hot dogs and that's tasty, too. This recipe can also be doubled or tripled if you're nervy enough to want to serve it for company. (I have, and let me tell you that there is never so much as one bean left in the pot.)

2 cans (about 16 oz. each) baked beans (see note)
1 large onion, chopped (1 cup)
⅔ cup unsulphured molasses
⅔ cup catsup
8 frankfurters, each cut diagonally into 3 pieces

Preheat oven to 300°F.
Butter a 2- to 2½-quart casserole and set aside.
Mix baked beans, onion, molasses, catsup, and frankfurter pieces in a large bowl. Spoon into prepared casserole, making sure that all the pieces of frankfurter are pushed well down into the baked beans.
Bake for 1½ to 2 hours, or until mixture is thick.
MAKES 6 TO 8 SERVINGS.
Note: For this casserole, use the most ordinary baked beans on the supermarket shelf. I don't know why they work better than the fancier brands, but they do.
Heart-preserver tip: Choose frankfurters that are reduced in fat and eat just one.

Philly Cheese-Steak Sandwich

Displaced Philadelphians pine for this sandwich that is as much a part of the city as William Penn's statue and soft pretzels with mustard. Even though the popularity of the cheese-steak sandwich is spreading nationwide, Philadelphians say they just don't taste the same outside the city limits. Part of the secret of a good cheese-steak sandwich is the restaurant griddle on which they're cooked, and that's hard to duplicate at home. You don't have to be Philly born to learn to love these!

2 hard rolls, each measuring about 6 x 3 inches (or you can use a
   loaf of Italian or French bread, measuring about 12 x 3
   inches, cut in half)
4 tablespoons butter
1 large onion, thinly sliced and slices separated into rings
2 frozen thin-sliced sandwich steaks (do not thaw)
6 slices American cheese
Salt and pepper to taste

Preheat oven to 200°F.

Cut rolls not quite through and open them up like a book.

Melt 1 tablespoon of the butter in a large, *nonstick* skillet. When sizzling, place one of the split rolls, cut side down, in the skillet. Weight down with another skillet and cook for about a minute. Remove roll from skillet. Add another tablespoon of butter to the skillet and repeat with remaining roll. Place rolls in the oven to keep warm.

Add another tablespoon of butter to the skillet. When it is bubbly, add onion and cook, stirring, over medium heat until lightly browned. Remove from skillet and set aside.

Add remaining tablespoon of butter to the skillet. When it sizzles, add steaks and cook over high heat, turning once, until browned. Lay 3 slices of the cheese over each steak. Cover pan to heat and melt cheese.

Place cheese-topped steak in the center of each of the rolls. Place reserved onion on top of steaks. Season with salt and pepper. Close sandwiches and serve immediately with potato chips and dill-pickle slices.

MAKES 2 SERVINGS.

Heart-preserver tip: Toast unbuttered rolls under the broiler; reduce the amount of butter called for when cooking onion and steaks; substitute a low-fat American cheese.

Canned-Corn Corn Pudding

Like most American families of a certain era, mine was more than a little fond of starchy foods. So corn made frequent appearances on the table all year round. In the summer we ate my father's corn from the vegetable garden and in the winter my mother made this wonderful corn pudding once or twice a week. (In those carefree days corn never took the place of potatoes at a meal, either. Serve them, too, if you want.)

1 can (about 16 oz.) cream-style corn
1 egg, lightly beaten
2 tablespoons melted butter
1 tablespoon all-purpose flour
1/4 teaspoon salt
1/8 teaspoon pepper
1 to 3 teaspoons sugar

Preheat oven to 350°F.

Butter a 1-quart casserole and set aside.

Mix corn, egg, butter, flour, salt, and pepper in a medium bowl. Add sugar to taste. Turn into prepared casserole.

Bake, covered, for 30 to 40 minutes, or until a knife inserted in the center comes out clean.

MAKES 4 SMALLISH SERVINGS (TWO CORN-PUDDING LOVERS COULD POLISH THIS OFF EASILY).

Heart-preserver tip: Omit butter.

The Ubiquitous (and Delicious!) Three-Bean Salad

In my opinion, modern-day bean salads can't hold a candle to the original. They are simply too healthful (not enough sugar and oil; strange beans and sprouts) to be considered at all soothing.

1 can (about 16 oz.) cut green beans
1 can (about 16 oz.) cut wax beans
1 can (about 16 oz.) kidney beans (buy a quality brand so that the
    beans will be firm and bright red)
1 or 2 medium onions, thinly sliced and the slices separated into
    rings
1 or 2 carrots, very thinly sliced
3 ribs celery, finely chopped
1 small green pepper, cored, seeded, and finely chopped
    (optional)
⅔ cup white vinegar
½ cup sugar
⅓ cup corn oil
1 teaspoon salt
1 teaspoon pepper

Thoroughly drain beans in a large colander.

In a large bowl, mix beans, onion, carrot, celery, and green pepper (if using).

In a small bowl, mix vinegar, sugar, oil, salt, and pepper, stirring until sugar is completely dissolved. Pour over vegetables and mix well.

Cover and chill for several hours, or overnight, before serving.

If kept tightly covered in the refrigerator, this salad will keep well for several days.

MAKES ABOUT 8 CUPS.

Heart-preserver tip: This one is okay for your heart.

Smashed Potatoes

These often took the place of mashed potatoes and were quite daring for their day. (God forbid we should ever have eaten a potato skin.) They are still great with hamburgers or other plain fried or broiled meats, mealtime mainstays on Saturdays nights, as well as every other night in the week. Since these potatoes were served with plenty of melted butter, gravy wasn't necessary.

1½ to 2 lbs. all-purpose potatoes
4 tablespoons butter, cut into pieces
Salt and pepper

Scrub potatoes and cut them into big pieces. Cover by a couple of inches with generously salted water. Boil, covered, until fork-tender. Drain well, then immediately smash lightly with a potato masher or fork. Drop butter into saucepan and season with salt and pepper to taste. Cover and set aside for a couple of minutes until the butter has melted. Stir and serve.

MAKES 4 SERVINGS.

Heart-preserver tip: Reduce butter, or substitute with margarine.

Almost Potato Chips

In her neverending search to find acceptable mashed-potato substitutes, my mother often made these tasty baked potato slices, which always reminded me of potato chips, so, of course, that qualifies these for comfort food.

Slice unpeeled, all-purpose or baking potatoes no more than ⅛-inch thick (or they won't crisp up). Dip slices in melted butter and arrange on nonstick or lightly greased jelly-roll pans (*not* baking sheets; otherwise the butter will run off onto the bottom of the oven). Sprinkle with salt and pepper.

Bake at 375°F for about 35 minutes, or until golden and crisp. (Actually you can bake these at any reasonable temperature, depending on what else is in the oven at the same time, increasing or decreasing the baking time accordingly.)

Remove from pan with a wide spatula and serve *hot.*

And that's all there is to it!

Heart-preserver tip: Dip potatoes in melted margarine.

Oscar's Waldorf Salad

Anything from the Waldorf-Astoria Hotel was pretty fancy stuff back in the forties, but since the recipe was easy, as well as classy, we gobbled it down—and still do, because it's good, comforting food. Some moms added a handful of raisins, but the Waldorf version of the salad doesn't call for them. (Oscar, by the way, was the maitre d'hotel at the Waldorf, not the chef.) The Waldorf recipe doesn't call for sugar or milk, either, but they have become such accepted ingredients in the salad dressing that I included them here. Make the dressing first so that the apples won't have a chance to brown after you cut them. If for any reason you have to let them sit, toss them with a little lemon juice.

½ cup mayonnaise
1 teaspoon sugar, or to taste
1 to 2 teaspoons milk
2 crisp red apples (about 1 lb.)
2 or 3 ribs celery, finely chopped
Iceberg lettuce leaves
½ cup coarsely chopped walnuts

Mix mayonnaise and sugar to taste in a small bowl. Beat in milk to thin slightly. Set aside.

Core apples and cut into small cubes. Immediately toss apples and celery with mayonnaise mixture in a medium bowl.

Arrange lettuce leaves on individual salad plates. Spoon salad onto lettuce leaves and sprinkle with walnuts. Serve immediately.

MAKES 4 SERVINGS.

Heart-preserver tip: Substitute reduced-fat mayonnaise for regular mayonnaise.

Saturday-Style Ambrosia

For a recipe that's fat free (something comfort foods rarely are), this one really hits the spot when it's served with or after a rich and/or salty dish. Many ambrosia recipes call for the oranges to be segmented over a bowl, but the comfort-food cook, ever-anxious to get to the end result (like my mother), hardly has time for that. Just be sure to take enough time when you're peeling the orange to make sure that all the bitter white pith is removed from the orange before it's sliced.

(Most moms wouldn't have, but if you like you can sprinkle a little orange liqueur between the layers of oranges.)

6 small juicy oranges
1 can (3½ oz.) flaked coconut
1 cup miniature marshmallows
A few maraschino cherries, cut in half

With a small, sharp knife, cut away the peel and bitter white pith from the oranges. Cut oranges into thin slices and the slices in half, removing seeds.

Place half the orange slices in a 2-quart serving bowl. Cover with half the coconut and half the marshmallows. Repeat these three layers. Cover tightly and refrigerate for several hours, or overnight.

Just before serving, scatter cherries over top.

MAKES ABOUT 6 SERVINGS.

Heart-preserver tip: This one is okay for your heart, but you might want to cut down on the coconut a bit.

Shredded Carrot and Raisin Salad

Green wasn't a big color for salads back when I was growing up. Except for summertime when there was garden lettuce, I rarely remember eating it. Canned string beans and peas were more likely to be served, which is probably why so many of us have vivid memories of the sweet crunchiness of this and the Waldorf salad.

¾ pound small carrots
½ cup dark raisins, or to taste
Mayonnaise
Iceberg lettuce leaves

Scrape carrots, then cut into shreds on a four-sided grater or, better, a food processor. You should have about 3 cups.

Mix shredded carrot, raisins, and mayonnaise to taste, in a medium bowl.

Arrange salad leaves on individual salad plates. Pile carrot mixture on top of lettuce.

MAKES 4 SERVINGS.

Heart-preserver tip: Substitute reduced-fat mayonnaise for regular mayonnaise.

Tomato-Cheese Rarebit

Similar to a Welsh Rabbit (or rarebit), this has variously been called Blushing Bunny, Red Devil, and other silly names through the years. Besides Creamed Hard-Boiled Eggs, it is one of the few meatless main dishes, for which I have fond and lasting memories.

1 can (10¾ oz.) condensed tomato soup
¼ cup milk
1 cup (4 oz.) shredded pasteurized process cheese spread loaf
*   (Velveeta!)*
8 to 12 slices buttered toast, cut into triangles
8 slices bacon, crisp-cooked and crumbled

Stir together soup, milk, and cheese in a medium-size saucepan. Cook over medium heat, stirring often, until cheese is melted and mixture is hot.

Divide toast among 4 to 6 plates. Spoon rarebit over toast. Sprinkle with crumbled bacon.

This tastes good with a glass of milk or a glass of beer, depending on your mood. And the addition of a modern-day green salad makes it a nice supper dish.

MAKES 4 TO 6 SERVINGS.

Heart-preserver tips: Use skim milk; unbuttered or margarine-buttered toast; skip the bacon.

Creamed Hard-Boiled Eggs

When I was growing up, well-stocked grocery stores closed at the dot of five o'clock. (After all, what else did women have to do all day but get their food shopping done early?) So, if for some reason you found yourself with a nearly bare refrigerator you were out of luck, except maybe to buy a quart of milk and a loaf of bread at some renegade mom-and-pop store. This, then, was what my mother frequently served on the occasions when we returned late in the day from my father's numerous business trips on which we often accompanied him. I think I find this dish comforting because it always reminds me of how happy I was to come home and be reunited with my Dalmatian dog, Patches, even though it took a while for the house to heat up in those days of the balky coal furnace.

You can make a large, creamy serving of this dish for one (yourself) by using *two* eggs and *half* the cream-sauce mixture.

6 large eggs
1/2 teaspoon dry mustard
4 tablespoons all-purpose flour
4 tablespoons butter
2 cups milk
Warm buttered toast triangles or cooked rice
Paprika, for garnish

Place eggs in a large saucepan and cover with a couple of inches of cold water. (You can first prick the more rounded end of each egg with a pin or a little device made expressly for this purpose, which will help keep the eggs from cracking as they boil.) Bring to a boil over medium-high heat. The moment the water starts to boil, remove the eggs from the heat, cover tightly, and let stand for *exactly* 20 minutes. Rinse with cold water and peel. Cut eggs into large pieces and set aside.

Mix mustard with flour on a piece of wax paper and set aside.

Heat butter in a large saucepan over medium heat until sizzling. Add flour mixture and cook, stirring constantly, until bubbly. Stir in milk all at once. Continue to cook and stir until mixture boils and thickens. Continue to cook and stir for 1 minute. Gently stir in eggs.

Serve over warm buttered toast triangles or rice. Sprinkle with paprika, if you like.

MAKES 4 SERVINGS.

Heart-preserver tips: Substitute oil or margarine for butter, and skim milk for whole milk; serve on unbuttered or margarine-buttered toast.

The Original Pudding Cake With Carol's Buttercream Frosting

It's my recollection that this cake suddenly appeared in the late fifties and has been going strong ever since. It's even available as a cake mix, although I can't imagine why since the original is so easy to make—and so much better, to my taste, anyway. My mother came home with the recipe one day about thirty years ago. She'd eaten the cake in a restaurant and somehow persuaded the owner to tell her how to make it.

Under ordinary circumstances, pudding cake is rich enough to serve plain, sprinkled with confectioners' sugar, with a scoop of ice cream, but if you are baking it for comfort, you may want to go all the way and cover it thickly with Carol Gelles's irresistible frosting.

1 package (about 18 oz.) yellow cake mix
1 package (4-serving size) instant vanilla pudding
4 eggs
¾ cup vegetable oil
¾ cup sherry (any kind but cooking sherry, which contains salt)
1 teaspoon ground nutmeg

FROSTING:
1 box (16 oz.) confectioners' sugar
¾ cup butter, softened (6 tablespoons)
½ cup sour cream
2 teaspoons vanilla extract
¾ teaspoon white vinegar
⅛ teaspoon salt

Preheat oven to 350°F.
Grease and flour a 10-inch tube pan and set aside.
Place cake mix, pudding, eggs, oil, sherry, and nutmeg in the large bowl of an electric mixer. Beat at low speed until ingredients are

combined, then at medium speed for 5 minutes. Turn batter into prepared pan.

Bake for 50 minutes to 1 hour, or until a wooden pick inserted in the center comes out clean.

Cool cake in the pan on a wire rack for about 30 minutes. Turn out of pan onto rack to cool completely.

To make frosting, place sugar, butter, sour cream, vanilla, vinegar, and salt in the large bowl of an electric mixer. Beat at low speed until combined. Increase speed to high and beat for 3 minutes, or until frosting is light and fluffy.

Thickly frost cooled cake, making the usual dips and swirls with a long icing spatula, and being sure to get the frosting all the way down into the hole in the middle.

MAKES 10 TO 12 SERVINGS.

Heart-preserver tip: Serve without Carol's frosting, thank you very much.

Sugar Pie

For my taste, this may be one of the best recipes in the whole book, and one of the most soothing. My mother (you'll remember that she never makes anything that takes much time), has been baking it for years and can't even remember where she got the recipe. It *must* be served warm and is sweet, *sweet,* but that should not deter you from serving it with a scoop of vanilla ice cream or whipped cream. Refrigerate leftovers and reheat before serving again. I can assure you that you will be asked for this recipe many times, and will then receive many phone calls around dinnertime from those to whom you gave the recipe who have misplaced it and want to serve it for company. Once eaten, this is a pie that is not forgotten.

3 eggs
2 cups firmly packed dark-brown sugar
4 tablespoons melted butter
1 unbaked 9-inch pie shell.

Preheat oven to 350°F.

Beat eggs and brown sugar with a wire whisk in a medium-size bowl until smooth and no lumps remain. This may take a couple of minutes. Stir in butter until well blended. Pour into unbaked pie shell.

Bake on a cookie sheet for 45 to 50 minutes, or until a knife inserted in the center comes out clean.

MAKES ABOUT 8 TO 12 SERVINGS.

Heart-preserver tip: This serving should be about $\frac{1}{16}$ of the circumference of the pie. No ice cream or whipped cream, either.

Tomato Soup Cake

This recipe originally came out of the Campbell's Soup test kitchens and it has been a real winner. Traditionally, the Tomato Soup Cake is lavishly covered with cream cheese frosting, which sort of makes you think you're eating something healthful.

2 cups all-purpose flour
1⅓ cups sugar
4 teaspoons baking powder
1 teaspoon baking soda
1½ teaspoons ground allspice
1 teaspoon ground cinnamon
½ teaspoon ground cloves
1 can (10¾ oz.) condensed tomato soup
½ cup solid white vegetable shortening
2 eggs
¼ cup water
Confectioners' sugar (optional)

CREAM CHEESE FROSTING:
2 packages (3 oz. each) cream cheese, softened
1 box (16 oz.) confectioners' sugar
½ teaspoon vanilla extract

Preheat oven to 350°F.

Generously grease and flour two 8- or 9-inch layer cake pans, or one 13 x 9 x 2-inch baking pan, or a 2½-quart (10-inch) Bundt pan. Set aside.

Measure flour, sugar, baking powder, baking soda, and spices into the large bowl of an electric mixer. Add soup and shortening. Mix on low speed to blend ingredients. Continue to beat at medium speed for 2 minutes (300 strokes by hand), frequently scraping bottom and side of bowl. Add eggs and water. Beat 2 minutes longer, scraping bowl frequently. Scrape batter into cake pans.

Bake layers or baking dish for 35 to 40 minutes, or until a wooden pick inserted in the center comes out clean. Bake Bundt-pan cake for 1 hour. Let stand in cake pans or baking dish for 10 minutes on a wire rack. Remove from pans or baking dish and cool completely on rack. Cool Bundt-pan cake right side up in pan for 15 minutes. Remove from pan and cool completely on a wire rack.

To make frosting, beat cream cheese in a large bowl until smooth. Gradually blend in sugar and vanilla. If necessary, thin with a little milk to give a good spreading consistency.

Frost cooled cake with cream cheese frosting, or simply dust with confectioners' sugar.

MAKES 16 SERVINGS.

Heart-preserver tip: No matter how healthful Cream Cheese Frosting sounds, it's not heart food. Stick with a thin slice of plain cake, dusted with confectioners' sugar.

Gooey Baked Apples

Baked apples can be a pretty dull scene, but not if you're making them as comfort food. That means with lots of nuts and raisins, plenty of brown sugar and butter, and, finally, a big spoonful of warm, brown-sugar-sweetened cream to top everything off. My father liked to spoon sweetened condensed milk on his apples. Perhaps you'd like to try that. There's nothin' better.

½ cup firmly packed dark-brown sugar
½ teaspoon ground ginger
4 tablespoons butter, softened
¼ cup finely chopped pecans or walnuts
2 tablespoons raisins
4 large Golden Delicious or other baking apples, peeled

TOPPING SAUCE:
1 cup whipping cream
2 tablespoons dark-brown sugar

Preheat oven to 350°F.

Mix brown sugar, ginger, and butter in a small bowl. Stir in nuts and raisins and set aside.

Core apples, making sure the hole is big enough to accommodate plenty of the filling, but being careful not to cut through the bottom of the apple. Place apples in a shallow baking pan just large enough to hold them comfortably.

Spoon brown-sugar mixture into apples, mounding slightly at the top, if necessary.

Bake for 50 to 60 minutes, or until apples are fork-tender.

While apples are baking, bring cream and brown sugar to a simmer in a small saucepan. Cook over medium-low heat, stirring frequently, until thick, about 20 minutes. Serve warm or chilled.

Remove apples from oven. Serve warm or chilled with cream topping.

MAKES 4 SERVINGS.

Heart-preserver tip: Skip the topping; reduce or omit butter in the filling, or substitute with margarine.

Coffee-Marshmallow Cream

I think my mother (and everybody else) got this recipe out of a box of marshmallows. In those days, marshmallows were packed in little blue boxes, divided by a sheet of waxed cardboard that had recipes printed on it. If ever a recipe was passé, it's this one. But it sure does make good comfort food.

24 regular-size marshmallows
¾ cup strong black coffee
1 cup whipping cream

Mix marshmallows and coffee in a large saucepan. Bring to a simmer over medium-high heat. Lower heat and simmer, stirring frequently, until the marshmallows are melted. Cool to room temperature.

Whip cream until stiff peaks form when beaters are lifted.

Fold whipped cream into marshmallow mixture. Spoon into 6 dessert glasses or a serving bowl. Chill until set.

MAKES 4 TO 6 SERVINGS.

Heart-preserver tip: This isn't very good heart food. Keep the servings miniscule.

Whipped Cream Refrigerator Cookies

The original version of this recipe (Famous Chocolate Refrigerator Roll) has appeared on the side of the box of Nabisco chocolate wafers, with which it was originally made, for at least 30 years, so you don't need me to repeat it. However, any recipe that has so endured must be garnering the approval of a whole new group of food shoppers every ten years or so. I just want you to know that the method works well for almost any kind of cookie, homemade or store-bought, that you like.

One evening after a dinner party, I had a little sweetened whipped cream left over and, rather than throw it out, I mixed it with a few gingersnaps I had sitting on the counter to make sort of a tiny trifle. The next day I tried it. Wow!

For each 6 oz. of cookies you will need 1 cup of whipping cream whipped with 1 or 2 tablespoons of confectioners' sugar. Place a few cookies, broken in half, in the bottom of a medium-size bowl and spread with whipped cream. Continue in this manner, layering the cookies with the whipped cream, ending with whipped cream on top. Cover tightly and refrigerate for several hours, or overnight.

Spoon into serving dishes.

MAKES 4 TO 6 SERVINGS.

Heart-preserver tip: This is *not* a heart-preserver recipe, so indulge in only a small spoonful or two.

IV SEMI-ETHNIC SOOTHERS:
Too-Sweet Spaghetti
Sauce and Other
Krafty Delights

When I was a little girl, I loved to leaf through my mother's two cookbooks, which included a few, dinky black-and-white food pictures, as well as some larger pictures of four-legged stoves. One photo I particularly remember showed two lamb chops, a little pile of peas, and some mashed potatoes on a plain plate.

As quaint as that picture seems now, it was actually quite a good example of the way Americans ate before World War II. There were, of course, the Mama Leones and others like her cooking Italian in New York and Chicago, thousands of Scandanavians in Minnesota serving *lutefisk,* and a few Chinese here and there wokking up chow mein, but most Americans were simply too far from their roots to cook anything like the food of their mother countries.

It was the U.S. troops returning from Europe with stories of the food they'd tasted overseas that started the ethnic-food ball rolling. Certainly these men were responsible for at least one enduring Italian favorite: pizza. Americans were still a long way away from cooking anything that reasonably resembled authentic foreign food, and our idea of it (much of which came straight off the Kraft Playhouse), would probably have horrified a native of its country of origin.

Nevertheless, these recipes are now a part of the history of American cooking, and many of them, some ridiculously farfetched, are firmly etched in our minds as comfort food.

Carol Gelles's Mother's Chopped Chicken Liver

"When I was young," Carol says, "before the wonderful world of the food processor, we used to put the livers through a hand-cranked grinder. It was my job to turn the crank until my arm was numb. To add to my discomfort, Mom always attached the grinder to an old step ladder, which would dance around the room as I cranked, and the trick was not to let the bowl of ground liver fall on the floor.

"My mother insisted that the liver be ground twice, and, in truth, it probably had a more uniform consistency and a bit more 'tooth' to it than the food processor can ever quite achieve. But, then again, maybe my memory isn't quite as faithful as I'd like to think it is, either."

Carol says her mom liked to make her chopped liver "eggy," and the use of mayonnaise instead of schmaltz (rendered chicken fat) was almost a sacrilege. Nevertheless, Carol's mom's chopped liver is the best we've ever tasted.

1/4 cup vegetable oil
2 large onions, chopped (2 cups)
*1 lb. chicken livers, rinsed and any fat or tough membranes
    discarded*
4 hard-cooked eggs, peeled and cut into quarters
1/3 cup mayonnaise
1 1/2 teaspoons kosher salt, or to taste
1/4 teaspoon pepper

Heat oil in a large skillet over medium-high heat. Add onion and cook, stirring, until golden. Stir in livers and continue to cook, turning and moving the livers around in the pan, until they are no longer pink in the center, about 7 minutes. Set aside to cool completely.

Place cooled liver mixture and eggs in the work bowl of a food processor fitted with a steel blade. Process until liver and egg mixture is fairly smooth. Scrape into a medium-size bowl.

Stir mayonnaise, salt, and pepper into liver mixture. Adjust seasonings to your own taste.

Serve with crackers, bread, or raw vegetables.

MAKES 2½ TO 3 CUPS.

Heart-preserver tip: This is not heart-healthy food. Eat at your own risk, and certainly just a little.

An American Grandmother's Lasagna

What would an American grandmother of English-Irish-German descent know about lasagna? Almost nothing. Nevertheless, on a gray day *this* is the lasagna of choice for many of us.

1 lb. lean ground beef (such as sirloin or round)
1 medium onion, chopped (½ cup)
1 can (6 oz.) tomato paste
1½ cups water
2 teaspoons salt
1 teaspoon dried oregano
½ teaspoon garlic powder
¼ teaspoon pepper
½ lb. lasagna noodles, cooked and drained as package directs
1 container (15 oz.) ricotta cheese
2 packages (6 oz. each) sliced mozzarella cheese
¼ cup grated Parmesan cheese

Preheat oven to 375°F.

Generously grease a 12 x 8-inch lasagna pan and set aside.

Brown ground beef in a large skillet over medium-high heat, stirring and breaking up with the side of a spoon, until lightly browned. Remove to a small bowl with a slotted spoon and set aside.

In the fat remaining in the skillet, cook onion over medium heat, stirring, just until softened. Return meat to skillet. Stir in tomato paste, water, salt, oregano, garlic powder, and pepper. Cover and simmer 30 minutes, stirring now and then.

Layer noodles, meat mixture, ricotta cheese, and mozzarella cheese in the prepared pan. Sprinkle with Parmesan cheese.

Bake for 30 minutes, or until top is lightly browned and mixture is bubbling around sides of pan.

Cool for 5 to 10 minutes before cutting and serving.

MAKES 4 TO 6 SERVINGS.

Heart-preserver tip: Low-fat ricotta and mozzarella cheeses may be substituted for the whole-milk varieties.

Welsh Rabbit (or Rarebit, if you prefer)

It's doubtful that Mother, or Grandmother, thought of this as "foreign" food when she prepared it for light suppers or to tempt an invalid's appetite. But foreign it is, a dish originally created by Welsh women to tease their husbands when they came home empty-handed from the hunt. Undoubtedly what the Welsh ladies' cooked up was less insipid than this old-fashioned American version, and would probably have been made with a stout ale and a good English Cheddar. Be that as it may, when we're feeling poorly, this is the rabbit (or rarebit) we so fondly remember.

> *2 tablespoons butter*
> *4 tablespoons all-purpose flour*
> *⅛ teaspoon salt*
> *Big pinch dry mustard*
> *Pinch ground red pepper*
> *¼ teaspoon Worcestershire sauce*
> *1½ cups milk*
> *1 cup shredded American cheese (4 oz.)*
> *Toast triangles, toasted English-muffin halves, or crackers*

Melt butter in the top of a double boiler over simmering water. Stir in flour, salt, dry mustard, red pepper, and Worcestershire sauce. Add milk all at once. Cook, stirring constantly, until smooth and thickened. Stir in cheese. Continue to cook, stirring occasionally, until cheese is melted and mixture is hot.

Serve over toast triangles, toasted English-muffins, or crackers.

MAKES 2 OR 3 SERVINGS.

Heart-preserver tips: Substitute low-fat milk for whole, and use low-fat American cheese.

North-of-the-Border Chili with Beans

My father-in-law, Tom Garrison, used to make huge pots of this stuff and invite everybody over to help eat it. The accompaniments were always plenty of saltines and plenty of beer. Lately I have been sprinkling my chili with chopped raw onion, shredded Monterey Jack (or Cheddar) cheese, and sour cream. (Obviously, I have been influenced by the great influx of Tex-Mex restaurants in New York.) If you're in no mood to invite a crowd in for dinner, you can cut this recipe in half and put away leftovers to enjoy another day. (You have no idea how fantastic this chili will taste after it has languished in the refrigerator for a few days.)

3 lbs. lean coarse-ground beef (such as sirloin or round)
2 or 3 medium-size onions, chopped
1 big red or green bell pepper, chopped
2 cloves garlic, minced
½ teaspoon oregano
¼ teaspoon cumin seed
2 cans (6 oz. each) tomato paste
4 cups water
Salt
Pepper
2 or 3 tablespoons chili powder
2 cans (about 15 oz. each) undrained kidney beans

Cook ground beef in a Dutch oven or other large, heavy sauce pot until lightly browned, stirring constantly. Add onion, red or green pepper, garlic, oregano, and cumin seed, stirring until mixture is well blended. Stir in tomato paste, then water. Add a couple of teaspoons of salt, a liberal grinding of pepper, and, for starters, 2 tablespoons chili powder.

Simmer for about an hour and a half, then stir in undrained beans. Simmer for another 30 minutes or so. During this last 30 minutes of cooking, add more salt, pepper, and chili powder to taste.

Remove from heat and set aside to cool. Refrigerate for several hours, at least, to allow flavors to mellow and blend. Reheat when ready to serve.

MAKES 8 GENEROUS SERVINGS.

Heart-preserver tip: Reduce amount of meat used to as little as 1½ lbs. Actually, this is not bad heart food.

Corn Chip and Chili Pie

This is Great American Junk Food at its finest: fatty and salty. But, oh, how it hits the spot on certain occasions. Accompany with a tall, icy Coke.

1 bag (8 oz.) corn chips
1 large onion, chopped (1 cup)
1 cup shredded Cheddar or Monterey Jack cheese (4 oz.)
2 cans (15 oz. each) hot-style chili with no beans

Preheat oven to 350°F.

Sprinkle 2 cups of the corn chips in a 2-quart baking dish. Sprinkle onion and half the cheese on top of chips. Cover with chili. Top with another cup of corn chips and remaining cheese.

Bake for 10 to 20 minutes, or until bubbly.

MAKES 4 TO 6 SERVINGS.

portable corn chip and chili pie:

Split an individual-size bag (3½ oz.) of corn chips down one side. Add 3 or 4 tablespoons chili, a little chopped onion, and some shredded cheese. Eat hot or cool.

Heart-preserver tip: These are *not* heart-healthy foods.

Caesar Salad

There are at least 50 cute and interesting stories about how and where this salad originated, but it all had to do with a bus load of stranded people and a restaurant in Northern Mexico, or maybe it was Southern California. (In the case of the latter, this would not be "foreign" food, but it always seemed so to me.) No matter. Caesar salad has been an American property for many years, usually ordered at a restaurant and often prepared by the waiter at tableside. Caesar salad went out of fashion for a long time and it became a rarity to see it offered. Now it's back on the menu—and at ridiculous prices, I might add. Making a Caesar salad at home is fun, not much trouble, and will take your mind off your troubles.

CROUTONS:

1 large clove garlic, peeled and quartered
1 cup olive oil
1 loaf French bread

SALAD:

1 large clove garlic, put through a garlic press
½ teaspoon salt
¼ teaspoon freshly ground pepper
1, 2, or 3 anchovies or up to 1 tablespoon anchovy paste (optional)
Few drops Worcestershire sauce
1 fresh unblemished egg
¼ cup olive oil
8 cups firmly packed romaine lettuce leaves that have been torn into bite-size pieces, dry and chilled (a large head of romaine should do it)
1 small lemon, cut in half and as many seeds as possible removed with the tip of a knife
2 to 4 tablespoons freshly grated Parmesan cheese

Several hours before you plan to serve the salad, start the croutons by dropping garlic into olive oil. Set aside for several hours.

To make croutons, remove crust and cut remaining bread into ¾-

inch cubes, or whatever size you like them. Spread cubes out on a sheet of wax paper to allow the bread to dry out a bit, then it won't absorb so much of the oil when you fry it.

Remove garlic from oil. Pour about half of the oil in a large skillet. (A nonstick skillet works well for this.) When it is very hot, add about half of the bread cubes and cook over medium-high heat, turning constantly, until lightly browned. Remove to paper towels to drain. Repeat with remaining oil and bread cubes.

The dressing for the salad can be made a little in advance of serving, if that's more convenient. Place garlic and salt in the bottom of a large salad bowl. With the back of a wooden, salad-serving spoon, mash the garlic and salt until they are pasty. Add pepper, anchovies, and Worcestershire sauce and continue mashing and stirring with the back of the spoon until well mixed and fairly smooth. Stir in egg until well blended, then start adding oil in a very thin stream, stirring furiously with the back of the spoon, until the mixture thickens.

Right before serving (at tableside, we should hope), add romaine to the salad bowl and toss until each leaf glistens. Squeeze the juice from the lemon halves (or to taste) over lettuce and toss again. Sprinkle with Parmesan cheese and toss briefly.

Divide salad among 4 large salad plates or between 2 dinner plates. Arrange croutons on top and add a grinding of pepper.

MAKES 2 TO 4 SERVINGS.

Heart-preserver tip: Since recent studies have shown that olive oil is good for your heart, go ahead and enjoy a reasonable-size serving.

Stuffed Shells

This is another of Grandma's ideas of what Italian cooking should be. Depending on the brand of spaghetti sauce you buy, you might want to add a little oregano and garlic to spice things up a bit more. If your name ends in a vowel, you might want to go on to the next recipe.

3 eggs
1 container (15 oz.) ricotta cheese
1 cup shredded mozzarella cheese (4 oz.)
½ cup grated Parmesan cheese
¼ cup chopped parsley
½ teaspoon salt
¼ teaspoon pepper
24 jumbo pasta shells
1 medium-size onion, chopped (½ cup)
2 tablespoons chopped green bell pepper
2 tablespoons olive oil
1 can (16 oz.) whole peeled tomatoes, undrained
1 jar (about 15 oz) red meatless spaghetti sauce

Grease a 13 x 9 x 2-inch baking dish and set aside.

Beat eggs in a medium-size bowl. Stir in ricotta and mozzarella cheeses, and ¼ cup of the Parmesan cheese until blended. Stir in parsley, salt, and pepper and set aside.

Cook shells in boiling, salted water for about 10 minutes, or until tender. Be careful not to overcook or the shells will tear. Drain *thoroughly*.

Preheat oven to 400°F.

While shells are boiling, cook onion and green pepper in oil in a medium-size saucepan until soft. Stir in tomatoes, breaking up with the side of a spoon. Add spaghetti sauce and remaining ¼ cup Parmesan cheese. Bring to a simmer, stirring, and keep warm.

Stuff shells, using a heaping tablespoon of the cheese filling for each one. Arrange in prepared baking dish. Pour warm sauce over and around filled shells.

Bake, uncovered, for 20 minutes, or until sauce is bubbly.

MAKES 6 SERVINGS.

Heart-preserver tip: Substitute low-fat riccotta and mozzarella cheeses for the whole-milk varieties.

Sort-of Beef Stroganoff

The classic version of Stroganoff calls for tender strips of pricey beef tenderloin, beef broth, a small amount of sour cream, and not much else, and is served over rice. However, when our mothers got hold of the recipe, sometime in the mid-fifties, all that changed. Mom substituted cheaper cuts of beef (even hamburger) and the Stroganoff was on its way to being turned into a hearty American meat stew, thickened with mushroom soup and *lots* of sour cream, a dairy product that skyrocketed to fame and popularity once dried onion soup was added to it. Alas, it is this latter version that we pine for when we want something creamy and good over noodles.

3 tablespoons butter
1 lb. sirloin steak, cut into strips measuring about 3 x ½ x ½
  inches
1 large onion, chopped (1 cup)
1 large clove garlic, minced
1 can (4 oz.) sliced mushrooms
1 can (10¾ oz.) cream of mushroom soup
½ pint sour cream
¼ cup chopped parsley
6 cups cooked wide noodles (12 oz. dry)

Melt 1 tablespoon of the butter in a large skillet. When it is bubbly, add half the meat and cook over high heat, stirring and tossing, until seared on the outside, but still pink and juicy on the inside. Remove from the skillet to a bowl with a slotted spoon. Cook remaining meat in another tablespoon of butter. Remove from skillet to bowl and set aside.

Add remaining tablespoon of butter to skillet. Stir in onion and garlic and cook over medium heat, stirring constantly, until golden. Stir in undrained mushrooms and soup and bring to a boil. Reduce heat and stir in sour cream, then reserved meat. Cook, stirring constantly, until heated through. After the sour cream is added, do not let the mixture boil or it will curdle.

Sprinkle with parsley and serve over hot noodles.

MAKES 4 TO 6 SERVINGS.

Heart-preserver tip: Not highly recommended.

Shrimp Scampi

Actually, scampi means shrimp in Italian, and I'm sure you all know that, but back in the carefree days, when we wanted great, big shrimp, sizzling in butter, oil, and garlic, and sprinkled with parsley, we asked for "shrimp scampi." This is it. This is what you remember. Serve it with generous chunks of crusty Italian bread to sop up the juices.

1 lb. large shrimp
3 tablespoons melted butter
3 tablespoons olive oil
2 tablespoons fresh lemon juice
2 large cloves garlic, put through a garlic press
¼ teaspoon coarsely ground pepper
¼ teaspoon cracked red pepper (optional)
¼ cup chopped parsley
Crusty Italian bread

Preheat oven broiler.

Shell shrimp and devein (that means to make a shallow slit in the back of the shrimp and remove the black line with a small, sharp knife). Rinse briefly in cool water and pat dry on paper towels.

Combine melted butter, olive oil, lemon juice, garlic, black pepper, and cracked red pepper (if using) in a medium-size bowl. Add shrimp and toss to coat with the oil mixture. Arrange shrimp in a shallow, broiler-proof dish large enough to hold them in a, more or less, single layer. Pour over remaining oil mixture.

Broil 4 to 5 inches from source of heat for about 2 minutes. Remove from broiler and turn shrimp over. Return to oven and broil for about 1 ½ minutes longer, being careful not to overcook.

Serve, sizzling from the broiler, sprinkled with parsley and garnished with lemon wedges.

MAKES 2 OR 3 SERVINGS, DEPENDING ON HOW MUCH BREAD YOU EAT AND WHAT ELSE YOU SERVE WITH THE SHRIMP.

Heart-preserver tip: Substitute margarine for butter and limit the size of your serving.

Creamy Roquefort Dressing

Since Roquefort cheese comes only from France, that makes this ethnic food, right? Well, at least *I* always thought of it as foreign when I graduated to it from Granny's Russian dressing and iceberg lettuce.

½ cup mayonnaise
⅓ cup crumbled Roquefort cheese
¼ teaspoon crushed garlic (optional)
1 tablespoon light cream, half-and-half, or milk
½ teaspoon Worcestershire sauce
⅛ teaspoon salt
Pinch white pepper

Mix mayonnaise, cheese, and garlic in a small bowl. The mixture should not be completely smooth. In other words, there should still be identifiable bits of cheese in the dressing. Beat in cream, Worcestershire sauce, salt, and pepper.

Simply wonderful over any kind of greens you like—even iceberg lettuce.

MAKES ABOUT 1¼ CUPS.

Heart-preserver tip: Substitute reduced-fat mayonnaise for the regular variety; thin out with skim milk to taste.

Spaghetti and Meatballs

In my house, nobody ever bothered to make the tomato sauce that accompanied these meatballs and spaghetti. My mother simply used a large jar (about 32 oz.) of really gutsy, red tomato sauce. If you are fortunate enough to have a few meatballs and some sauce left over, you will want to have a fattening meatball sandwich the next day.

TOMATO SAUCE:
1 tablespoon olive oil
1 large onion, chopped (1 cup)
1 large clove garlic, minced
1 can (28 oz.) whole tomatoes, undrained
1 cup water
1 can (6 oz.) tomato paste
1 teaspoon sugar, or to taste
1 teaspoon dried oregano
½ teaspoon salt
¼ teaspoon pepper

MEATBALLS:
1 lb. lean ground beef (such as sirloin or round)
¼ cup dry, unflavored bread crumbs
¼ cup grated Parmesan cheese
1 small onion, minced (¼ cup)
2 tablespoons chopped parsley
1 clove garlic, put through a garlic press
1 egg
½ teaspoon salt
⅛ teaspoon pepper
2 tablespoons olive oil
Hot cooked spaghetti (about 1 lb.)

Heat oil in a Dutch oven or other large, heavy sauce pot. Add onion and garlic and cook, stirring, over medium-high heat until softened. Stir in tomatoes, water, tomato paste, sugar, oregano, salt, and pepper. Reduce heat and simmer, uncovered, for about 1 ½ hours, or until sauce has thickened to the consistency you like. Stir occasionally during cooking, breaking up the tomatoes as much as possible with the side of a spoon.

To make meatballs, gently mix ground beef, bread crumbs, cheese, onion, parsley, garlic, egg, salt, and pepper in a large bowl. Use your hands for the mixing job, or a wooden salad-serving fork works well. Shape mixture into 1½-inch meatballs.

Heat oil in a large skillet. When it is hot, add meatballs and cook quickly over medium-high heat to brown on all sides.

About 20 minutes before sauce is done, add meatballs.

(The sauce will be considerably improved if you allow it to mellow for a day or so in the refrigerator before it is served.)

Place hot, drained spaghetti on a large platter. Spoon tomato sauce with meatballs over spaghetti.

Serve immediately with additional Parmesan cheese.

YIELDS 4 CUPS SAUCE, 16 MEATBALLS.

Heart-preserver tips: Fill up on spaghetti and go light on the meatballs and sauce.

Meatball Sandwiches

You can also use these meatballs and tomato sauce to make nifty meatball sandwiches.

Arrange 3 or 4 meatballs and some of the sauce on long, split rolls. Top with provolone cheese, if you like.

Baklava

Those people who grew up in cities with a Greek population of any size will doubtless have fond recollections of this sweet-sweet-sweet Greek dessert. Some of us have only discovered it in the past few years, and promptly added it to our ever-growing repertoire of cloying comfort foods.

I cannot imagine what it would be to make baklava from scratch—
or at least before the days of frozen, paper-thin, phyllo dough, but the
availability of this handy product has certainly made Ms. Zorbas out of
Ms. O'Briens and all the rest of us.

> *1 bag or can (16 oz.) finely chopped walnuts*
> *½ cup sugar*
> *1 teaspoon ground cinnamon*
> *1 package (16 oz.) phyllo dough (strudel leaves), thawed as*
> *   package directs*
> *1 cup butter, melted (2 sticks)*
> *1 jar (12 oz.) mild honey*

Preheat oven to 300°F.

Butter a 13 x 9-inch baking dish and set aside.

Mix walnuts, sugar, and cinnamon in a large bowl until well
blended and set aside.

Remove thawed phyllo from package and unfold.

(*This is important!*) While working with phyllo dough, keep those
sheets that you are not immediately working with covered with damp
paper towels. Otherwise they will dry out and flake away.)

Place one sheet of the phyllo dough in the prepared dish. Brush
lightly with melted butter. Repeat this procedure to make four more
layers of phyllo and butter for a total of five layers. Sprinkle evenly
with 1 cup of the walnut mixture.

Place one sheet of phyllo over the walnut mixture and brush lightly
with melted butter. Repeat to make five layers as before. Sprinkle with
another cup of the walnut mixture.

Repeat layering two more times for a total of four layers, ending
with phyllo. Brush the final layer of phyllo with remaining butter. With
a very sharp knife, cut just *halfway* through the layers of phyllo and
filling into triangles. (Start by cutting into 12 rectangles, then cut the
rectangles into 24 triangles.) This precutting is done because the top of
the baklava will simply be too crumbly to cut after it is baked.

Bake for about 1 hour and 30 minutes, or until the top is golden
brown.

Heat honey in a small saucepan over medium-low heat.

As soon as baklava is removed from the oven, spoon hot honey over it so that the honey will be absorbed into the layers of phyllo and filling as it cools. Cool completely on a wire rack. Cover and leave at room temperature until ready to serve.

To serve, finish cutting through the layers.

MAKES 24 SERVINGS.

Heart-preserver tip: Substitute margarine for butter.

Creme Caramel

Happy was the day when we discovered that the creme caramel we relish at French restaurants was really little more than the baked custard we loved as nursery food.

1 cup sugar
4 eggs
¼ teaspoon ground nutmeg
Pinch of salt
2 cups half-and-half
1 cup milk
1 teaspoon vanilla extract

Preheat oven to 350°F.

Place ½ cup of the sugar in a small, heavy skillet and heat gently until the sugar melts and turns pale golden. Begin stirring and stir constantly until the sugar syrup turns to a deep golden color. Be careful not to let it get too dark. Immediately spoon 1 tablespoon of the caramel into each of six, 6-oz. custard cups. Set aside while mixing custard.

In a medium-size bowl, stir eggs just until blended. Stir in remaining ½ cup sugar, nutmeg, and salt until well mixed.

Heat half-and-half and milk in a heavy, medium-size saucepan until very warm. Gradually stir into egg mixture. Stir in vanilla.

Place prepared custard cups in a shallow baking pan just large enough to hold them comfortably. Pour custard into cups, dividing evenly. Pour about 1 inch of hot water into the larger pan.

Bake for 30 minutes, or until a knife inserted in the center of one of the custards comes out clean.

Immediately remove custard cups from hot water. Let custard stand at room temperature until cool, then cover and chill for at least several hours before serving.

To serve, run a sharp knife around the edge of each custard to loosen. Invert a serving plate on top of the custard cup and invert together. Remove cup. Voila!

MAKES 6 SERVINGS.

Heart-preserver tip: As wholesome and comforting as this is, it is not exactly what the cardiologist ordered. Eat only on good or bad special occasions.

V

QUICK PICK-ME-UPS FOR SUDDEN LETDOWNS

The high-powered salesman who didn't close the deal . . . One more frazzled working mother trying to gather the mental and physical strength to tackle the laundry or help with the homework after a manic Monday. Since a quick session with the therapist is out, they reach for a chocolate-covered graham cracker, or some other fast food that will provide instant emotional relief.

When time is short, but the need is great, a quick-to-fix comfort food can be almost as soothing as a mother's hug.

Instant Relief Fudge

Although the desire for fudge usually strikes at odd hours, whipping up a reasonably tasty batch needn't be a big deal. This fudge doesn't really compare with Mamie's Million Dollar version on page 169, or Aunt Ruth's Opera Fudge on page 186, of course, but, on the other hand, you are likely to have all these ingredients on the shelf, and it only takes 15 minutes from the time the craving strikes until you can plop a big piece into your mouth.

4 tablespoons butter
3 squares (1 oz. each) unsweetened chocolate
½ cup light corn syrup
1 tablespoon water
1 teaspoon vanilla extract
1 box (16 oz.) confectioners' sugar
½ cup chopped nuts or 1 cup miniature marshmallows (optional)

Butter an 8-inch square pan and set aside.

Melt butter and chocolate together over low heat in a heavy, medium-size saucepan. Stir in corn syrup, water, and vanilla. Remove from heat and *immediately* stir in confectioners' sugar, and nuts or marshmallows (if using). The mixture will be quite stiff.

Pack into a prepared pan. Cool and cut into squares.

MAKES ABOUT 1¾ LBS.

Heart-preserver tips: There are none. Fudge is not heart-healthy food.

Finger-lickin' Good, Chocolate-Coated Marshmallows and Pretzels

The mindless act of dipping pretzels or marshmallows into smooth, glistening chocolate is almost as soothing to the psyche as actually eating the finished product. Just be sure to keep enough of your mind on the business at hand so that you do not get so much as a drop of water into the melted chocolate, which will turn it stiff as a board.

Once you've chocolate-coated marshmallows and pretzels, and realize the potential of the procedure, you will be dipping all sorts of things: crackers, cookies, nuts, fresh and dried fruits, for instance. Even Chinese fried noodles. Graham crackers, strawberries, and dried apricots take particularly well to a chocolate bath.

Finely chopped nuts (optional)
6 oz. semisweet or milk chocolate, broken or chopped into small
  pieces
1 tablespoon solid white vegetable shortening
Regular-size marshmallows
Thin pretzels, measuring about 3 inches at their widest point

Lay pieces of wax paper over two large baking sheets and set aside. Place chopped nuts (if using) on a sheet of wax paper and set aside.

Melt chocolate with shortening in the top of a double boiler over hot, *not boiling,* water. Remove from heat and stir until smooth.

Remove top of double boiler and dry bottom before setting on work area.

With a dinner fork, dip marshmallows or pretzels into chocolate. Lift out, then tap the handle of the fork on the side of the pan so that excess chocolate will drip back into the saucepan. Roll in chopped nuts, then arrange, not touching one another, on prepared baking sheets. When all marshmallows or pretzels have been coated, place sheets in the refrigerator until chocolate hardens, 15 to 20 minutes.

Remove from wax paper and store in a cool spot, the refrigerator probably being the best place. For even when kept in a so-called cool spot, unless you're a very fast eater, the chocolate coating will begin to melt on your fingers almost instantly.

THIS RECIPE MAKES ENOUGH CHOCOLATE TO COAT ABOUT 20 MARSHMAL-LOWS, OR 16 TO 18 PRETZELS.

Heart-preserver tip: The marshmallows and pretzels are okay, but go easy because the chocolate and shortening are not!

Home-on-the-Range Marshmallows

I think my mother must have been a saint to let me do this, and *I* must have been a saint to let *my* kids do it. But we did. We toasted marshmallows in the fireplace. I guess it was easier than building a campfire.

Marshmallows toasted in the oven just don't do it for me. The procedure for toasting marshmallows in the fireplace is about the same as toasting them over a fire: a long, wet, pointed stick with a marshmallow firmly skewered onto the end.

Toasting marshmallows over a gas burner requires only a kitchen fork and about 5 seconds of your time.

Believe me, a toasted marshmallow will take you right back to some of the nicest times in your life: camping days and family picnics.

Heart-preserver tip: These are fat-free!

S'mores

Now that you know how simple it is to toast marshmallows over the gas burner, you can sneak downstairs on a sleepless night and fix yourself this old pajama-party favorite.

1 graham cracker, broken in half
1 milk-chocolate or semisweet chocolate bar, the same size as the
    graham cracker, broken in half
1 or 2 hot toasted marshmallows

On top of the graham-cracker half, place a chocolate-bar half. Smoosh one or two toasted marshmallows on top of the chocolate.

Eat immediately while the marshmallow is still hot and gooey.

Heart-preserver tip: Indulge moderately.

Sugar-and-Butter Sandwiches

This simple, open-faced sandwich helped get me through the long nights at boarding school when I didn't like what was served for dinner—which was most nights. Since there was always bread, butter, and sugar on the table, the rest followed naturally.

1 slice squishy white bread
Softened butter
Sugar

Generously spread bread with butter, being careful not to tear the bread. Generously sprinkle with sugar. There should be enough butter and sugar on the bread to ooze through your front teeth when you bite into it.

Heart-preserver tip: Substitute margarine for butter, and go light on it.

Cheese Fries

Frozen French fries make this salty little treat a reality any time you get a craving.

Melt pasteurized process cheese spread loaf *(Velveeta!)* in a double boiler or microwave oven while fries are heating.

Pour *hot* melted cheese to taste over *hot* fries. This should be much too hot to eat when you take your first bite.

Heart-preserver tip: Salty and fatty. Extreme discretion advised.

Milk Toast, Sweet and Savory

The ultimate comfort food. Perfect for perfectly rotten days.

2 slices white, whole-wheat, or rye bread slices
Softened butter
1 cup hot milk
Salt and pepper to taste

Toast the bread, then butter it and break up into a shallow bowl. Pour hot milk over toast and sprinkle with salt and pepper to taste.

Sweet Milk Toast

Sprinkle prepared toast with sugar or cinnamon-sugar to taste before adding hot milk. Omit salt and pepper.

Cheesy Milk Toast

Sprinkle prepared toast with a little bit of very finely shredded American or Cheddar cheese before adding hot milk. Sprinkle with pepper to taste.

Heart-preserver tips: Substitute skim or low-fat milk for whole milk; be spartan when spreading with butter, or use margarine.

Blender Eggnog

Eggnog was something special that Mother shook up (in a ridged container especially designed for mixing up shakes of all kinds) whenever she thought we were looking pale or peaked, and it sure as heck beat a tablespoon of cod liver oil, the tonic *she* took as a tot. Whenever you're feeling out of sorts or not up to snuff, remember that it takes only about a minute and a half to whip up an eggnog that can usually be counted on to have you back in good mental shape in no time.

> *1 fresh unblemished egg*
> *1 to 2 tablespoons sugar*
> *¼ teaspoon vanilla extract*
> *1 cup milk*

Place egg, sugar, and vanilla in the container of an electric blender. Blend until mixture is thick and pale. Add milk and blend on high speed until frothy.

Pour and feel better.

MAKES ABOUT 1¼ CUPS.

Heart-preserver tip: Substitute skim or low-fat milk for whole milk.

Heavenly Deviled Eggs

Once upon a time, we thought of eggs as only being good for you, and we were urged by Mom and Granny to eat as many as we liked. One of the ways they tempted us was with deviled eggs, which could often be found ready and waiting in the refrigerator (in a covered glass refrigerator tray) any time we hungered for a savory snack. In moderation, eggs are still good for you. If you can wait long enough to boil an egg, a smooth, creamy, deviled egg can work psychological wonders.

1 large egg
¹/₁₆ teaspoon prepared yellow mustard
Few drops white or cider vinegar
Few grains sugar
Pinch salt
Pinch pepper
Mayonnaise
Paprika, for garnish

Prick the large end of the egg with a pin. (This may help to keep it from cracking as it boils.) Place egg in a small saucepan and add enough water to cover by a couple of inches. Bring to a boil. Immediately remove from heat. Cover tightly and let stand for *exactly* 20 minutes. Drain and then let cold tap water run over egg until it can be handled comfortably.

Tap egg gently over a hard surface, then start peeling from the large end. Rinse under cool water and pat dry on paper towels.

Cut egg in half lengthwise and carefully scoop out the yolk (being careful not to tear the white) into a small bowl. Mash the still-warm yolk with the back of a table fork. Add mustard, vinegar, sugar, salt, and pepper. (The amounts listed are only intended as a guide. Taste as you go.) Continue to mash and stir until smooth and well blended. Stir in just enough mayonnaise to make a good stuffing consistency.

With a teaspoon fill egg halves with the yolk mixture, mounding the tops slightly.

Sprinkle with paprika.

A deviled egg, when being eaten for comfort, should never be consumed in more than four bites.

Heart-preserver tip: Eggs will be eggs! Don't forget to count this one as part of your weekly allotment.

SODA-FOUNTAIN TREATS

New York Chocolate Egg Cream

For those people brought up in any of the five boroughs of New York, this is true comfort food. For New Yorkers, the ingredients and preparation of this basically simple drink are more like a religious service, so intent are they in making sure that what they are about to drink is a true copy of the egg creams they remember as a child. They even go so far as to order seltzer in special bottles and a special chocolate syrup (in commercial gallon containers) that each is convinced is the actual chocolate syrup that was used in the egg cream of their dreams.

Even if you're from Alaska or Iowa, you're bound to like this refreshing drink, which is, more or less, an ice cream soda without the ice cream.

2 to 4 tablespoons chocolate syrup, chilled
¼ cup light cream or milk
Seltzer water or club soda, chilled

Spoon syrup into a big, tall glass. Briskly stir in cream with a long spoon. Slowly add seltzer, pouring down the side of the glass, stirring furiously.

Drink *immediately*.

MAKES ONE, LONG SATISFYING EGG CREAM.

Black-and-White Ice Cream Soda

To turn the chocolate egg cream into an ice cream soda, combine 1 scoop of vanilla ice cream, 2 tablespoons chocolate syrup, and ¼ cup milk (optional) in a tall glass. Stir to blend. Fill glass two-thirds full with seltzer or club soda. Stir gently. Place another scoop of vanilla ice cream and top off with a little more seltzer. Set another scoop of vanilla ice cream on the rim of the glass so that the ice cream just touches the seltzer, but does not fall down into it.

A Good-Old-Days Chocolate Milk Shake, Malted or Plain

For most of us over the age of thirty-five, the so-called milk shake one buys these days bears no resemblance whatsoever to the milk shake of the good old soda-fountain days. You could *drink* those milk shakes! They were created, while you watched, by a soda-fountain jerk who scooped the ice cream, flavorings, and milk into a tall metal container and hooked it precariously to the front of a beater. The frothy shake was then poured into a tall glass, and, as if he'd made a mistake in the measuring, the soda jerk always gave you what was left in the frosty container. (Soda-fountain etiquette dictated that you did not drink from the container!)

2 scoops chocolate ice cream (about ½ cup)
2 tablespoons chocolate syrup
1 to 2 tablespoons malted milk powder (leave this out and you
    have a plain chocolate milk shake)
1 cup milk

Place ice cream, syrup, malted milk powder, and milk in the container of an electric blender. Blend on high speed until frothy. Pour into a tall glass and drink with two straws.

MAKES ABOUT 2 CUPS.

Strawberry Malted Milk Shake

Substitute strawberry preserves for the chocolate syrup, and strawberry ice cream for chocolate ice cream, and there you have it.

Black-and-White Milk Shake

Use 4 tablespoons (or to taste) chocolate syrup, and substitute vanilla ice cream for chocolate ice cream.

The C.M.P.

The initials stand for chocolate, marshmallow, and peanut sundae, and there were two versions we could get at the little store at the crossroads in Pocono Pines, Pennsylvania, where I went to summer camp. Because they're so fattening, I think about these more often than I actually eat them these days, but just *thinking* about a C.M.P. transports me back to that little store with the pinball machine and Hank Williams and Tony Bennett singing their hearts out endlessly on the juke box.

VERSION I

1 or 2 scoops chocolate ice cream
Marshmallow cream
Chopped peanuts
Sweetened whipped cream
A maraschino cherry

Place a scoop or two of chocolate ice cream in a shallow bowl. Cover generously with marshmallow cream. Sprinkle with lots of chopped peanuts. Add a generous portion of whipped cream and top everything off with a maraschino cherry.

VERSION II
1 or 2 scoops vanilla ice cream
Marshmallow cream
Gooey Chocolate Sauce (page 188)
Chopped peanuts
Sweetened whipped cream
A maraschino cherry

Place a scoop or two of vanilla ice cream in a shallow bowl. Cover with marshmallow cream, then chocolate sauce. Sprinkle with lots of chopped peanuts. Add a generous portion of whipped cream and top everything off with a maraschino cherry.

As the marshmallow cream gets cold, it will develop a wonderfully chewy texture.

Dusty Road (Dusty Miller)

I must shamefully admit that during my boarding school days, I often skipped church in order to sit in the ice cream parlor on the corner and dawdle over a Dusty Road. I preferred mine without the whipped cream and the cherry.

1 or 2 scoops chocolate ice cream
Malted milk powder
Sweetened whipped cream
A maraschino cherry

Place ice cream in a shallow dish. Sprinkle with malted milk powder to taste. Cover with whipped cream and top with a cherry.

Hot-Fudge Sundae

2 scoops chocolate or vanilla ice cream
Gooey Chocolate Sauce (page 188), warmed
Sweetened whipped cream
Finely chopped walnuts
A maraschino cherry

Place 1 scoop chocolate or vanilla ice cream in a sundae glass and cover with warm Gooey Chocolate Sauce. Add another scoop of chocolate or vanilla ice cream. Top with more chocolate sauce, walnuts, and a maraschino cherry.

VI

BREAKFAST:
Morning, Noon, and Night

Breakfast is one of my favorite meals (I also have two others, depending on my mood). I suspect, like most things, it has to do with my childhood.

My father and I were both early risers, and because we were "morning people," more often than not we had the pleasure of each other's chatty company over the breakfast we ate in the kitchen on a maple drop leaf table that sat under the window. In my memory, the sun was always streaming in over the forsythia bushes, and beyond was the sledding hill that was either covered with snow or wildflowers. My dog, Patches, was always right there, hoping against hope that a piece of toast or sticky bun would drop on the floor. It always did.

We each cooked our own breakfast. Mine never varied much: hot cocoa (from scratch) and a scrambled egg that I cooked in a small, black iron skillet. (In thinking back, I realize that I had seasoned that old skillet so perfectly, the eggs never stuck to it.) Our old-fashioned toaster required that the bread be hand-turned after it was done on one side, and it burned more often than not. Fortunately, we liked burnt toast. I still do.

In those days, milk was delivered to the back door and came in glass bottles with cardboard caps. In the winter, it sometimes froze and the cream on top would push the cap off as it rose into a tall cone. If my mother had not yet come down, we would gleefully spoon some of the frozen cream off into little bowls and eat it. (Believe me, I get chest pains just *thinking* about that little trick.)

Nowadays, I don't often have time for the luxury of a home-cooked breakfast (in the morning, anyway) of scrambled eggs and a sticky bun. But when I do, I still sit down at the drop leaf table, and the sun still streams through the window. Although the view is very different, I still get that same "all's well" feeling that's so often part of a half-remembered childhood.

Strawberry Orange Juice

Perhaps you've been diluting frozen orange juice for so long that you've kidded yourself into believing that it actually tastes like the real thing, and have forgotten what a comfort drink fresh-squeezed orange juice can be.

May I suggest that you take the fresh juice one step further: For each 8 oz. of orange juice you will need 4 or 5 big, sweet strawberries, cut into halves or quarters. (Both oranges and strawberries, by the way, are now available year round, so you can make this drink any month your heart desires.)

Place orange juice and berries in the container of an electric blender or food processor. Blend or process until thoroughly mixed.

A little champagne won't hurt, either.

Fried Tomatoes with Cream Sauce

My father never drove—or took a train or a plane—if a ship or a boat was going in the same direction. On our annual automobile trips to Florida, he would circumvent at least part of the long, boring trip by booking passage on the Old Bay Line, a steamboat line that ran up and down the Chesapeake Bay ferrying passengers and cars between Baltimore and Norfolk. In the late afternoon we would drive aboard *The City of Richmond* or *The District of Columbia,* or one of the other sturdy little ships that comprised the fleet. After the car was tucked away in the hold for the night, we got a good night's sleep and, not incidentally, two wonderful meals. Memories of the dining saloon will always be a vivid one for me, where overhead fans moved the sea air about the spacious, quiet room. Food was served by white-jacketed waiters and tables were covered with white cloths.

Let me tell you, breakfast on the Old Bay Line was a far cry from anything my mother ever offered, and it may have been the first time I realized that this meal could be more than eggs, cereal, or toast. Grits, biscuits, sweet rolls, fried oysters, country ham, bacon, pancakes, waffles, and hot chocolate were among the many offerings we enjoyed, but the things I remember the most were fried tomatoes and fried apples.

It's been many years since the Old Bay Line succumbed to interstate highways and more efficient modes of transportation, but when I taste fried tomatoes or fried apples, I'm back in my carefree days, sailing on the Chesapeake Bay.

4 firm, slightly underripe tomatoes, each weighing about 8 oz.
Salt
Pepper
¾ cup all-purpose flour
½ cup bacon drippings (see note)
⅔ cup whipping cream

Cut a thin slice from the stem and blossom ends of each tomato, then cut tomatoes into ½-inch slices (4 slices per tomato). Sprinkle slices rather generously with salt and pepper. Spread flour on a piece of wax paper and dredge both sides of the tomato slices in it.

Heat bacon drippings in a large skillet over medium-high heat until sizzling. Lower tomato slices into drippings. Fry for about 2 minutes on each side, or until flour coating is nicely browned, adjusting heat as necessary. Frying will have to be done in two or three batches.

Place tomato slices on a platter as they are fried and keep them warm.

To make cream sauce, pour off drippings from skillet, but leave any brown particles that cling to the pan. Add cream, then cook and stir over medium heat for 2 or 3 minutes until cream simmers and thickens. Spoon over tomatoes and serve immediately.

MAKES 4 TO 6 SERVINGS.

Note: If you don't have any bacon drippings residing in a can in the back of the refrigerator, use half butter and half vegetable oil, or fry up some bacon and serve, crisp, with the tomatoes.

Heart-preserver tips: Use vegetable oil for frying tomatoes; serve without sauce, or substitute 1 can (5.3 oz.) of evaporated milk for the cream.

Fried Apple Rings

3 big apples, cored and sliced into ½-inch rings
2 teaspoons lemon juice
3 tablespoons sugar
¾ teaspoon ground cinnamon
2 tablespoons butter

Toss apple rings with lemon juice in a large bowl.

In a small bowl, combine sugar and cinnamon.

Melt 1 tablespoon of the butter in a large, nonstick skillet over medium heat. Add half of the apple rings, or as many as will fit in the skillet in a single layer. Sprinkle rings with about a third of the sugar mixture. Cook for 2 to 4 minutes, or until rings are half cooked, but still firm. Turn rings, sugared side down. Cook 2 to 4 minutes longer, or until cooked through, but still firm and sugar is melted. Lift with a pancake turner onto a platter, sugared side up, as they are fried, and keep warm. Frying will have to be done in two or three batches, adding more butter as needed.

MAKES 4 TO 6 SERVINGS.

Heart-preserver tip: Substitute margarine for butter.

Philadelphia Sticky Buns

Until recently, I hadn't eaten a really good sticky bun since we moved away from Eastern Pennsylvania over 30 years ago. Even the ones I get in Reading on visits don't seem to have the same soft, sticky consistency, nor are they loaded with the raisins and nuts that I remember so well. Not long ago I found what looked like an exceptional recipe for sweet dough and decided to give it a try. At first taste there was something hauntingly familiar about its taste and aroma, and suddenly it all came back to me: trips with my mother to the little bakery on Franklin Street and the wonderful, breakfast sticky buns she bought there once or twice a week. Just when I thought I'd never taste another wonderful sticky bun, I had it—the perfect dough in which to envelop the raisins, nuts, sugar, butter, and cinnamon for the sticky bun of my dreams.

Despite the length of this recipe, it is not difficult, especially if you have worked with yeast breads before. However, it is important to be precise and to follow the instructions to the letter.

I am delighted to be able to share this sticky bun recipe with you. It is my ultimate comfort food.

SWEET DOUGH:
1 1/2 cups water
1/3 cup sugar
1/3 cup solid white vegetable shortening
4 1/4 cups all-purpose flour
1 package active dry yeast
1 1/2 teaspoons salt
2 eggs

TOPPING:
1 cup firmly packed dark-brown sugar
4 tablespoons butter
2 tablespoons light corn syrup
1 tablespoon water
1 1/2 teaspoons white vinegar
1 1/2 cups chopped pecans (6 oz.)

FILLING:

2 tablespoons melted butter
¾ cup firmly packed dark-brown sugar
1 teaspoon ground cinnamon
½ cup raisins (optional)

In a 1-quart saucepan over high heat, stir together water and sugar until sugar is dissolved. Bring to a boil and boil over high heat for 3 minutes. Remove from heat. Stir in shortening and let stand for 30 minutes.

In a large bowl, stir together 2 cups of the flour, yeast, and salt. Stir in cooled sugar mixture, then eggs. Stir in 1½ cups more of the flour. Turn onto a well-floured board and knead for 7 minutes, using as much of the remaining ¾ cup flour as necessary until the dough is just slightly sticky. (If you've kneaded in all of the flour and are finding that the dough is still too sticky to knead easily, lightly dust your hands with additional flour, but don't add any more flour to the dough.)

Place dough in a greased bowl, turning the dough to grease the top. Cover with plastic film and leave in a warm, draft-free spot until doubled in bulk, about 1½ hours. Punch down and allow to rise again, about 40 minutes.

Grease the bottom and sides of a 9 x 13 x 2-inch baking pan.

Place brown sugar, butter, syrup, water, and vinegar in a 1-quart saucepan. Bring to a rapid boil, stirring until the sugar is dissolved. Boil for 1 minute. Pour into prepared pan. Sprinkle evenly with nuts and set aside.

Preheat oven to 375°F.

Roll dough into an 18 x 14-inch rectangle. Brush with melted butter. In a small bowl, stir together brown sugar and cinnamon. Sprinkle this mixture evenly over the dough. Sprinkle with raisins (if using). Roll from a long side and seal by pinching edges together. Slice into 12 pieces. Place over topping in pan, a cut side down.

Cover pan with plastic film and let rise until doubled in bulk, about 30 minutes. Remove plastic film.

Bake for about 25 minutes, or until browned.

Remove from oven and let stand 5 minutes. Turn onto a rectangular serving dish and eat right away.

MAKES 12 FABULOUS STICKY BUNS.

Note: Another time you can make these buns with a sugar frosting (confectioners' sugar and enough milk to make a good spreading consistency) instead of the caramel topping. In that case, frost buns after they have cooled.

Heart-preserver tip: Whatever happens to you as a result of eating these sticky buns, it's worth it.

Popover Pancakes

This puffy little breakfast confection can't decide if it's a pancake or a popover, but it doesn't matter, because it's so satisfying and so easy to make, and tastes as good at midnight as it does in the morning.

4 tablespoons butter, melted
3 eggs
4 tablespoons all-purpose flour
1/2 cup milk
2 tablespoons fresh lemon juice
1/4 teaspoon salt
1/2 teaspoon ground nutmeg
Apricot jam
Confectioners' sugar

Preheat oven to 425°F.

Place 1 tablespoon of the melted butter in each of two, metal 9-inch pie plates and set aside.

Beat eggs in a medium-size bowl. Add flour, 2 tablespoons at a time, beating just until reasonably smooth after each addition. Beat in milk, remaining 2 tablespoons butter, lemon juice, salt, and nutmeg.

Place pie plates with butter in the preheated oven. Watch carefully until plates are hot and butter is sizzling, but not browned.

Immediately divide batter evenly between pie plates (about 3/4 cup each).

Bake for 10 minutes on the middle oven rack. Lower heat to 350°F. and bake for 5 minutes longer, or until the sides of the pancakes have risen slightly on the sides and are lightly browned.

Spread with jam. Cut into wedges and sprinkle with confectioners' sugar.

MAKES 2 TO 3 SERVINGS.

Note: Another time you might like to sprinkle the pancake with about ⅓ cup miniature chocolate chips after it has baked for the first 10 minutes. Finish baking as instructed above.

This is also wonderful with a fresh fruit topping. I like mine with a few lightly sugared, fresh peach slices. Add the fruit after the pancake is baked.

Fried Potatoes

In some homes (mine, for instance), a special weekend breakfast would not be complete if it weren't for a big spoonful of crispy fried potatoes alongside the eggs.

Like coffee, fried potatoes tend to smell better than they taste. The secret to great-tasting fried potatoes is plenty of onion, and be sure to keep stirring, cooking them long enough to make sure that some of the potatoes and onions are brown and crisp. And be sure to use waxy new potatoes for frying—they won't crumble up and turn to mush without browning, the way baking or all-purpose potatoes tend to do.

> 1 lb. new potatoes
> 2 tablespoons butter
> 2 tablespoons bacon fat or vegetable oil
> 1 large onion, chopped (1 cup)
> 1 small green pepper, finely chopped (optional)
> Salt and pepper to taste

Cook new potatoes in boiling water, covered, until just tender when pierced with the tip of a knife or a kitchen fork. Drain thoroughly. Peel the potatoes, if you want to, then set aside to cool.

Cut potatoes into quarters or eighths, depending on their size. (This can be done ahead.)

Heat butter and bacon fat in a large skillet. When it is sizzling, add onion and pepper and cook over medium heat, stirring frequently, until just starting to soften, about 2 minutes. Raise heat slightly, add potatoes and continue to cook, stirring, tossing, and scraping the skillet, until done as you like them. Sprinkle with salt and pepper (lots of pepper, please) and stir into potato mixture. Serve immediately.

MAKES 4 SERVINGS.

Quick Fried Potatoes

Substitute 2 cans (16 oz. each) canned, sliced potatoes, rinsed under cool running water and patted dry, for new potatoes. Break the potatoes up a little with the side of a spoon as they are cooking.

Heart-preserver tip: Substitute vegetable oil for butter and fat.

Sugar-and-Walnut-Filled Coffee Cake

I know and you know that it's possible to buy a perfectly acceptable coffee cake, but nothing gets them out of bed and down to the breakfast table quicker than the aroma of a home-baked coffee cake filling the house. This is one of my favorites. This one is moist, tender, and easy. You can even mix and chill the filling ingredients and measure out the dry ingredients the night before.

FILLING:
4 tablespoons melted butter
½ cup light-brown sugar
1 tablespoon flour
1 tablespoon ground cinnamon
¼ cup chopped walnuts

CAKE:
1½ cups all-purpose flour
1½ teaspoons baking powder
½ teaspoon salt
½ cup butter, softened (1 stick)
½ cup sugar
½ teaspoon vanilla extract
1 egg
½ cup milk
¼ cup walnut pieces, for topping

Make filling by mixing butter, brown sugar, flour, and cinnamon in a small bowl. Stir in walnuts and set aside.

Preheat oven to 350°F.

Grease an 8-inch square baking pan and set aside.

Mix flour, baking powder, and salt in a medium-size bowl with a wire whisk until light and thoroughly combined. (Using a wire whisk to blend the dry ingredients makes sifting unnecessary in this case.)

Beat butter, sugar, and vanilla in a large bowl until well mixed. Beat in egg. Beat in flour mixture alternately with milk.

Spread half the batter into the prepared pan. Spread evenly with filling mixture. Top with remaining batter, spreading it evenly to the edges of the pan. Top with walnuts.

Bake for about 45 to 50 minutes, or until a wooden pick inserted in the center comes out clean.

Cool in the pan. Cut into squares to serve.

MAKES 9 SERVINGS.

Heart-preserver tip: Substitute margarine for butter.

Company Scrambled Eggs

I used to scramble eggs with whipping cream (2 or 3 tablespoons whipping cream per two eggs, if you'd care to), on those mornings when I craved rich, creamy eggs, but now I scramble them a la Carol Gelles, who uses cream cheese to enrich hers. To further insure creaminess, cook the eggs very slowly, stirring constantly over low heat.

8 eggs
1 package (3 oz.) plain cream cheese or cream cheese with chives,
    chilled and cut into bits
3 tablespoons butter
Salt, to taste
White pepper, to taste (you can use black, but then you have
    those disconcerting little black specks in the eggs)

Beat eggs until well mixed in a medium-size bowl. Stir in cream cheese.

Melt butter in a large skillet over medium-low heat. When it is melted, add eggs. Cook, stirring constantly, until the eggs have reached a creamy consistency and the cream cheese is melted.

Serve immediately on warm plates.

MAKES 4 SERVINGS.

Heart-preserver tip: You can't have everything.

Upscale French Toast with Warm Praline Syrup

This is the way a French cook makes French toast. It is nothing like nursery French toast, and which one you want depends on your mood and how many people there are to share it with you. Do take the time to make the praline syrup, or at least heat whatever syrup you serve, if you decide that making praline syrup is too much trouble.

4 tablespoons melted butter
3 eggs, lightly beaten
⅔ cup milk
3 tablespoons sugar (optional)
¼ teaspoon vanilla extract
8 slices French or Italian bread, each 1-inch thick, cut on the
 diagonal

WARM PRALINE SYRUP:
¾ cup firmly packed dark-brown sugar
¼ cup light corn syrup
3 tablespoons water
Pinch salt
1 tablespoon butter
¼ cup finely chopped pecans

Preheat oven to 400°F.

Pour melted butter into a 13 x 9-inch baking dish, tilting the dish so that the butter covers the bottom.

Combine eggs, milk, sugar (if using), and vanilla in a flat dish that is large enough to hold all of the bread slices in a single layer. Soak bread slices in this mixture for 2 minutes. Turn and continue to soak until the bread has absorbed all of the egg mixture.

Place bread in the prepared dish in a single layer.

Bake for 15 minutes. Turn and continue to bake until golden, about 10 minutes.

Serve immediately with Warm Praline Syrup.

To make syrup, combine brown sugar, corn syrup, water, and salt in a small saucepan. Bring to a boil and simmer for 2 to 3 minutes, stirring occasionally. Remove from heat; stir in butter and pecans.

The syrup may be made in advance. Reheat gently before serving.

MAKES 4 SERVINGS; 1 CUP SYRUP.

Heart-preserver tip: Substitute margarine for butter and skim milk for whole milk when making French toast. Omit butter from syrup.

Deluxe Creamed Chipped Beef

Do not try to serve this to anyone who has ever served in the U.S. Armed Forces. Other than that, it's great. (And to think there's a whole generation out there, I have recently learned, that has never even *heard* of this homey, comforting food!)

1 package (2.5 oz.) sliced dried beef
3 tablespoons butter
3 tablespoons all-purpose flour
1½ cups milk
1 can (4 oz.) sliced mushrooms, drained
Toast triangles, waffles, a baked potato, mashed potatoes, rice,
*   noodles, etc.*
Few sprigs parsley, for garnish

Remove dried beef from package and separate into pieces. Place in a colander and rinse under warm water for 10 or 15 seconds to remove excess salt. (If you don't mind the saltiness you can skip this step and simply separate the beef into pieces.)

Melt butter in a large skillet. Stir in flour until completely blended. Add milk all at once, stirring constantly, until mixture bubbles and thickens. Stir in mushroom slices and beef. Continue to cook, stirring, until heated through.

Now comes the decision about what to serve this on. My own preference is a fluffy, baked potato (see page 19) or a crisp waffle. Garnish with parsley sprigs.

MAKES 2 SERVINGS.

Heart-preserver tips: Rinse the beef as directed above; substitute margarine for butter and skim milk for whole milk.

Creamy (Is There Any Other Way?) Grits

A few months ago I had breakfast in the Willard Room of the newly restored Willard-Intercontinental Hotel in Washington, D.C., and I thought I'd died and gone to heaven for sure. Since Washington is well below the Mason-Dixon line, of course there was grits on my plate. But such wonderful grits. Here is the recipe I ran right home and cooked up that's just about as good as the Willard's.

1³/₄ cups half-and-half
2 cups water
³/₄ teaspoon salt
³/₄ cup hominy grits (not the quick-cooking variety)
1 tablespoon butter
¹/₄ teaspoon white pepper

Place half-and-half, water, and salt in a heavy, medium-size saucepan (a nonstick pan works well for this) and bring to a boil. Slowly stir in grits. Return to a boil and reduce heat. Cook slowly over very low heat for about 20 minutes, watching carefully and stirring occasionally.

Stir in butter and pepper and serve immediately.

MAKES 8 SERVINGS.

Note: Leftover grits may be chilled and reheated, although you will have to add a little more half-and-half.

Heart-preserver tips: Substitute milk for half-and-half. Omit butter or substitute with margarine.

Pecan Waffles

Waffles are another little breakfast treat that you may have gotten used to in the frozen state. Every now and then be good to yourself and bake them from scratch. And, as long as you're going to the trouble, you might as well make them extra special by adding some chopped pecans to the batter.

1 1/2 cups all-purpose flour
1/4 cup sugar
2 teaspoons baking powder
1/2 teaspoon salt
2 eggs, separated
1 1/2 cups milk
1/4 cup vegetable oil
1/2 cup finely chopped pecans or walnuts
Softened butter
Warm Praline Sauce (see page 156)

Mix flour, sugar, baking powder, and salt in a medium-size bowl with a wire whisk until light and thoroughly combined. (Using a wire whisk to blend the dry ingredients makes sifting unnecessary in this case.)

Beat egg yolks in a large bowl until thick and pale. Stir in milk, oil, and flour mixture just until moistened. Stir in pecans.

In a small, grease-free bowl, beat egg whites until soft peaks form when beaters are lifted. Fold into batter.

Bake waffles according to the directions that accompanied your waffle iron, or use about 1 1/3 cups batter to make one 9-inch-square waffle.

Serve immediately with softened butter and Warm Praline Syrup.

MAKES THREE 9-INCH WAFFLES OR TWO 4-INCH WAFFLES.

Heart-preserver tips: Substitute low-fat milk for whole milk; spread with softened margarine.

VII

FOR HEAVY-DUTY BLUES:
Pure Chocolate

Chocolate. The quintessential feel-good food, this 500-year-old gift to civilization from the Aztec Indians may be the world's favorite flavor. (But also thank God for the Spanish, who got the idea early on of adding sugar to Montezuma's bitter brew.)

Chocolate can be as innocent as a child's birthday cake or as sexy as a champagne truffle. It is eaten in celebration almost as often as it is eaten to cure a bad case of the blues—or simply to make a good day even better. Chocolate lovers swear that the powers contained in the little *cacao* bean go a lot further than the special, sensual sensation of a good piece of chocolate melting in the mouth, leaving in its wake a feeling of serenity and supreme satisfaction.

When cooking with chocolate there are a couple of important things you would do well to keep in mind.

Always remember that chocolate is a bit temperamental and doesn't take well to sudden extremes of hot and cold. Melt it gently, either over hot (not boiling) water in a double boiler, or over *very low* heat in a heavy saucepan.

Also, make sure that the pan and stirring spoon are absolutely dry and be certain that there is no rising steam, for if even a drop of condensed moisture falls into the melting chocolate it will stiffen and be almost impossible to use. Rescue it by stirring in 1 to 2 tablespoons of solid shortening (*not* butter or margarine) until the chocolate becomes fluid again.

Buy a good brand of chocolate (not necessarily the most expensive) and store it in a cool, dry place. In the summer you may have to refrigerate some chocolate, but be prepared for a whiteish "bloom" to form on the outside when it is brought back to room temperature, which won't affect its taste or cooking properties at all.

Chocolate keeps well when tightly wrapped and properly stored. *Baking chocolate* can be stored on the shelf or in the refrigerator for up to two years and in the freezer for as long as five years. *Milk chocolate* can be stored on the shelf for about six months, in the refrigerator for up to one year, and in the freezer for two years. *Cocoa,* if it's stored in a tightly closed container, can be kept on the shelf almost indefinitely.

When choosing loose chocolate, take a tip from the experts and look for brightness and gloss as important keys to its quality.

Heart-preserver tips for chocolate recipes? Don't be silly. Chocolate may help to mend a broken heart, but most chocolate goodies should be eaten with a certain amount of restraint and discretion.

Now, let's get cooking. We diet tomorrow!

A Wickedly Delicious Chocolate Cake with Creamy, Dark Chocolate Frosting

There is little to say about this moist, dense chocolate cake that may be one of the best you've ever eaten, a little slice of paradise for the chocolate lover. Because it's so moist, it's not always easy to remove the layers from the cake pans, so be sure to take the time to line the pans with wax paper as directed, even though it seems like a big bother. The results are worth the trouble. Trust me.

1¾ cups all-purpose flour

2 cups sugar

¾ cup unsweetened cocoa powder

2 teaspoons baking soda

1 teaspoon baking powder

1 teaspoon salt

2 eggs

1 cup strong black coffee, cooled or 2 teaspoons instant-coffee granules dissolved in 1 cup boiling water, cooled

1 cup buttermilk

½ cup vegetable oil

1 teaspoon vanilla extract

Strawberry fans or raspberries, for garnish

Lightly sweetened whipped cream or vanilla ice cream (optional)

DARK CHOCOLATE FROSTING:

4 squares (1 oz. each) unsweetened chocolate

½ cup unsalted butter (1 stick)

½ cup evaporated milk (not condensed milk)

1 teaspoon vanilla extract

⅛ teaspoon salt

1 box (16 oz.) confectioners' sugar

Preheat oven to 350°F.

Use the bottom of one of two, round, 9-inch cake pans to trace and cut out two circles of wax paper. Grease the cake pans and insert the circles of wax paper in the bottom of each one. Grease the wax paper, then flour the wax paper and the insides of the cake pans. Set aside.

Combine flour, sugar, cocoa, baking soda, baking powder, and salt in the large bowl of an electric mixer. Add eggs, cooled coffee, butter-milk, oil, and vanilla. Beat on low speed just to combine, then beat for 2 minutes at medium speed. The batter will be quite thin.

Divide batter evenly between prepared cake pans.

Stagger cake pans on oven racks and bake for 35 to 40 minutes, or until a wooden pick inserted in the center of the layers comes out clean and cakes are just starting to pull away from sides of pans.

Immediately turn out of pans onto wire racks to cool completely. Peel off and discard wax paper.

To make frosting, melt chocolate and butter in a small, heavy saucepan, stirring frequently, over *very low* heat. Remove from heat and set aside.

Add evaporated milk, vanilla, and salt to confectioners' sugar in a medium-size bowl. The mixture will be thin. Stir in melted chocolate mixture and beat with a wooden spoon until frosting thickens to a spreading consistency.

Fill and frost cake, making long swirls and dips with an icing spatula.

Garnish cake with strawberry fans or raspberries and serve with lightly sweetened whipped cream if you must. (To make strawberry fans, lay one whole strawberry on its side. With a small, sharp knife, make several cuts through the berry, starting at the bottom, and going up to the hull, but not through it. Gently press berry out, still attached at the hull, to make a fan.)

MAKES ONE 9-INCH LAYER CAKE, 8 TO 12 SERVINGS.

Brownies!

"I'd walk a mile for a brownie," could very well be the American motto. Many of us *think* we remember the brownies our mothers baked (whether she actually did or not is unimportant) as being the best—the chewiest, the cakiest, the moistest, the chocolatiest, the nuttiest, or whatever. I have found this recipe for brownies to be just about right. At least nobody has ever refused one, nearly everyone takes seconds, and I am asked for the recipe so often that I keep copies of it on hand. Taken with a tall glass of milk they are simply *wonderful*.

4 squares (4 oz.) unsweetened chocolate
½ cup butter (1 stick)
4 eggs
2 cups sugar
1 teaspoon vanilla extract
1 cup all-purpose flour
¼ teaspoon salt
1½ cups chopped walnuts or pecans
Confectioners' sugar for dusting brownies (optional)

Preheat oven to 325°F.

Lightly butter a 9-inch-square baking pan and set aside.

Melt chocolate and butter together in a small, heavy saucepan, stirring frequently, over *very low* heat. Remove from heat and set aside to cool.

In the large bowl of an electric mixer, beat eggs until frothy. Gradually add sugar and continue beating until the mixture is thick and pale, about 5 minutes. Stir in cooled chocolate mixture and vanilla, then flour, salt, and nuts until completely blended. Scrape batter into prepared pan.

Bake on the middle oven rack for 1 hour. Cool in the pan on a wire rack.

If you like, you can dust the cooled brownies with confectioners' sugar. Or, if things are really bad and your chocolate craving really intense, smear them with half the recipe for frosting given for A Wickedly Delicious Chocolate Cake on page 165. Cut brownies into bars.

MAKES 18 1½ X 3-INCH BROWNIES.

Hot Fudge Pudding Cake

This old-fashioned pudding cake is easy to make and everybody loves it. It even makes its own warm chocolate sauce in the bottom of the pan as it bakes. That's the good news. The bad news is that it should be eaten while it's still warm and doesn't reheat all that well. So, be sure there are enough chocolate lovers on hand to finish it up right away—say two, besides yourself.

1 cup all-purpose flour
1¼ cups granulated sugar
2 teaspoons baking powder
6 tablespoons unsweetened cocoa powder
⅛ teaspoon salt
½ cup milk
2 tablespoons melted butter
1 teaspoon vanilla extract
1 cup chopped pecans or walnuts
½ cup firmly packed light-brown sugar
1 cup water
Vanilla ice cream or whipped cream

Preheat oven to 375°F.
Generously butter an 8-inch square baking pan and set aside.
Place flour, ¾ cup of the granulated sugar, baking powder, 2 tablespoons of the cocoa, and salt in a medium-size bowl. Mix with a wire whisk until light and thoroughly blended. (Mixing the dry ingredients with a whisk makes sifting unnecessary in this case.) Stir in milk, melted-butter, and vanilla. Add nuts and mix until well combined. Scrape batter into prepared pan.
Combine remaining ½ cup granulated sugar, brown sugar, and remaining 4 tablespoons cocoa in a small bowl. Sprinkle over batter in pan. Pour water over top. *Do not stir.*
Bake on the middle oven rack for 45 minutes, or until top is crusty.
Remove from oven and let stand for 15 minutes. Spoon into dessert

bowls, spooning sauce from the bottom of the pan over top. Offer scoops of vanilla ice cream or whipped cream.

MAKES 6 TO 8 SERVINGS.

Mamie Eisenhower's Million-Dollar Fudge (According to Cecily Brownstone)

You all remember Mamie, don't you? She was the wife of the charismatic general who was also our 34th President. (I never heard tell of it, but perhaps it was packages of Mamie's fudge from home, and Lucky Strikes, of course, that kept Ike going during the long, dreary years of World War II.)

2 cups sugar
1 can (5.3 oz.) evaporated milk (not condensed milk)
1 tablespoon butter
Pinch of salt
1 package (6 oz.) semisweet chocolate pieces (1 cup)
6 oz. (from two 4-oz. bars) sweet baking chocolate, cut into small pieces
1 jar (7½ oz.) marshmallow creme
1 cup coarsely broken walnuts

Butter an 8-inch square baking pan and set aside.

Combine sugar, evaporated milk, butter, and salt in a heavy, 2-quart saucepan. Cook over medium-high heat, stirring constantly, until mixture comes to a full boil. Boil 5 minutes, stirring constantly. Remove from heat. Add both kinds of chocolate, marshmallow creme, and nuts. Stir vigorously until the chocolate is melted and the mixture is a uniform color. Scrape into prepared pan. Cut cooled fudge into squares.

MAKES ABOUT 2½ POUNDS OF INCH-HIGH FUDGE.

Triple-Treat Chocolate Cookies

There are *three* kinds of chocolate in these easy drop cookies, and to say they are divine does not begin to describe the delights in store for you when you bite into one. Freeze these cookies, three or four to a zipper-top plastic bag, for a portable chocolate fix that is head and shoulders over some old candy bar.

6 squares (1 oz. each) semisweet chocolate
2 squares (1 oz. each) unsweetened baking chocolate
3 tablespoons butter
⅓ cup all-purpose flour
1 teaspoon baking powder
¼ teaspoon salt
2 eggs
2 teaspoons vanilla extract
1 cup sugar
2 cups (about 8 oz.) chopped pecans
6 oz. (from two 4-oz. bars) sweet baking chocolate, chilled, then
    chopped into small pieces.

Preheat over to 325°F.
Grease two baking sheets and set aside.
Melt semisweet chocolate, unsweetened chocolate, and butter together in a heavy, medium-size saucepan, stirring frequently, over *very low* heat. Remove from heat and set aside to cool slightly.
Mix flour, baking powder, and salt in a medium-size bowl with a wire whisk until thoroughly blended and set aside.
Place eggs and vanilla in the large bowl of an electric mixer. Beat at low speed until frothy. Gradually add sugar and beat at high speed until thickened. Add melted chocolate and beat at medium speed until well blended. Add flour and beat at low speed until well combined. Stir in nuts and small pieces of sweet chocolate.
Drop batter by heaping measuring tablespoonfuls about 2 inches apart onto prepared baking sheets, flattening each one slightly with the back of the spoon.

For a slightly chewy cookie, bake for 15 minutes, or until tops crack. For a crisper cookie, add 5 minutes of baking time. Remove from baking sheets and cool on a wire rack.

MAKES 24 TO 30 COOKIES.

Chocolate-Mayonnaise Cake

For fifty-one years this cake has been resurfacing and thrilling a whole new generation of chocolate lovers every time it does. The original mayonnaise cake was created by Mrs. Paul Price, the wife of a Hellmann's mayonnaise sales distributor. It contained chopped dates and walnuts, but otherwise was very similar to this updated version that can even be microwaved in about 10 minutes if you're in a real rush for a chocolate-cake fix.

Although mayonnaise might seem like a strange ingredient for a cake, it's actually an excellent substitute for shortening or butter, which are the more typical ingredients used to create a moist cake with a tender crumb.

(Don't worry. You won't actually taste the mayo.)

2 cups all-purpose flour
⅔ cup unsweetened cocoa powder
1¼ teaspoons baking soda
¼ teaspoon baking powder
3 eggs
1⅔ cups sugar
1 teaspoon vanilla extract
1 cup mayonnaise
1⅓ cups water

Preheat oven to 350°F.

Grease and flour the bottoms of two, 9-inch, round cake pans and set aside.

In a medium-size bowl, whisk flour, cocoa, baking soda, and baking powder together and set aside.

In a large bowl, with an electric mixer set at high speed, beat eggs, sugar, and vanilla until light and fluffy, about 3 minutes. Reduce speed to low and beat in mayonnaise until well blended. Add flour mixture in four additions alternately with water, beginning and ending with flour.

Divide batter evenly between prepared cake pans.

Stagger cake pans on oven racks and bake for 30 to 35 minutes, or until a wooden pick inserted in the center of the layers comes out clean.

Cool in pans on wire racks for about 10 minutes. Remove from pans to cool completely on racks.

Frost and fill as desired.

MAKES ONE 9-INCH LAYER CAKE; 8 TO 10 SERVINGS.

MICROWAVE METHOD:

Follow recipe as given above.

Line bottoms of two, 8 x 2½-inch, round, glass cake dishes with circles of waxed paper or microwave paper towels. Divide batter between prepared cake dishes.

Microwave one layer at a time. Place cake dish on an inverted pie plate in a microwave oven. Microwave at Medium (50 percent power) for 5 minutes. If cake appears to be rising unevenly, rotate dish. Microwave on High for 3 to 5 minutes longer, or just until cake begins to set up on the outer edge. Although the center may appear to be slightly soft, it will firm up as it cools.

Let cake stand directly on a countertop for 10 minutes. Remove from cake dish and cool completely on a rack.

Repeat with remaining layer.

Chocolate Mousse Loaf

Chocolate lovers will think they've died and gone to heaven for sure when they first taste this creamy treat. If you don't feel like fooling around with unmolding this from a loaf pan, it will taste as good if it's been turned into a bowl before it's chilled. Then simply spoon servings onto dessert plates and call it a mousse. Fresh strawberries or raspberries are nice to serve on the side and add a sort of "healthful" touch to a recipe that should otherwise carry a warning from the surgeon general.

> *1 cup butter (2 sticks)*
> *1 cup unsweetened cocoa powder*
> *1 cup sugar*
> *2 tablespoons strong coffee or espresso*
> *4 eggs, separated*
> *½ cup chopped pistachios or other nuts (optional)*
> *Fresh strawberries or raspberries (optional)*
> *Unsweetened whipped cream*

Lightly grease an 8 x 4-inch loaf pan. Line the bottom and sides with foil. Lightly butter the foil and set the pan aside.

Melt butter in a medium-size saucepan. Stir in cocoa, ¾ cup of the sugar, and coffee. Pour into a large bowl. Let cool slightly. Add egg yolks, one at a time, beating well with a wire whisk after each addition.

Beat egg whites in a small, grease-free bowl with an electric mixer until foamy. Gradually add remaining ¼ cup sugar, beating until stiff peaks form when beaters are lifted.

Using the same beaters (no need to rinse), beat the chocolate mixture until smooth and well blended.

Stir about one quarter of the egg whites into the chocolate mixture, then fold in the remaining whites until no streaks of white remain.

Spoon into prepared pan. Cover and chill for several hours, or overnight, or freeze for later use.

When ready to serve, gently loosen foil from sides of pan. Place a serving platter over the pan. Holding the pan firmly, invert the platter and the pan. Lift pan off loaf and carefully peel away foil. Pat nuts onto the top and sides of loaf with your hands.

Garnish platter with berries.

To serve, cut into reasonably thin slices (I know that may be hard to do, but this is *very* rich stuff) and offer whipped cream.

MAKES 12 SERVINGS.

Whoopee Pies

The world seems lopsidedly divided when it comes to whoopee pies. Mention them to a few people and they think you're talking dirty. Describe them to others, who will give you a glassy-eyed look and a guilty grin. *They* are the chocolate lovers who have experienced these Very Special Treats at one time or another in their lives, probably during childhood and perhaps under another name. No matter what it's called, once you have eaten a whoopee pie, you are not likely to forget it. If whoopee pies are not currently on your list of comfort foods, eat one and they soon will be.

This recipe makes about 20 pies, but you don't *have* to eat them all at once. You can wrap the pies individually in plastic film and freeze. Then, when the urge strikes, all you need do is retrieve one from the freezer! Let the pie thaw on the counter for a few minutes, or eat it frozen.

1 cup sugar
½ cup solid white vegetable shortening
2 cups flour
½ cup unsweetened cocoa powder
1½ teaspoons baking soda
1 teaspoon salt
1 cup milk
2 teaspoons vanilla extract

FILLING:
½ cup butter, softened (1 stick)
1 jar (7½ oz.) marshmallow creme
¾ cup confectioners' sugar
¼ cup solid white vegetable shortening
½ teaspoon vanilla extract

Preheat oven to 350°F.
Grease 3 or 4 baking sheets and set aside.
To make pies, beat sugar and shortening in the large bowl of an electric mixer until well blended.

Mix flour, cocoa, baking soda, and salt in a medium-size bowl with a wire whisk until light and thoroughly combined. (Using a wire whisk to blend the dry ingredients makes sifting unnecessary in this case.)

With an electric mixer running at low speed, add flour mixture and milk alternately to sugar mixture, starting and ending with flour mixture, beating well after each addition. Beat in vanilla.

Drop batter by heaping measuring tablespoonfuls 2 inches apart on prepared baking sheets. (The little cakes will be about 2½ inches in diameter after baking.) You should have about 40 cakes.

Bake for 15 minutes, or until cakes spring back when touched lightly. Remove to wire racks to cool.

While cakes are baking, prepare filling. In a large bowl, combine butter, marshmallow creme, sugar, shortening, and vanilla. Beat 2 minutes with an electric mixer at high speed until light and fluffy.

Place about 1 tablespoon filling on the flat sides of half the cakes. Top with remaining cakes and press together so that the filling squishes out the sides a little.

MAKES ABOUT 20 WHOOPEE PIES.

Note: Because of all the butter in the filling, these pies should not be held at room temperature indefinitely. Pies that are not to be eaten soon after baking should be wrapped in plastic film and refrigerated or frozen.

A Divinely Decadent Chocolate Cheesecake

Christine Loomis, chocolate lover and creator of this sublime cheesecake, says she makes the cake for holiday dinners and family reunions because they are the only times when enough people come to make a dent in it. "Too few people to help eat this means too much leftover chocolate cheesecake in my refrigerator," she says.

Author's note: How can there ever be "too much" leftover chocolate cheesecake?

3 bags (5½ oz. each) brownie chocolate-nut cookies
½ teaspoon ground cinnamon
10 tablespoons melted butter (1 stick plus 2 tablespoons)
1 cup sugar
3 packages (8 oz. each) cream cheese, softened
4 eggs
16 oz. semisweet chocolate, melted over very low heat and cooled
1 teaspoon vanilla extract
2 tablespoons unsweetened cocoa powder
2 cups sour cream

Crush cookies to a fine, even crumb in the container of an electric blender or food processor. (You can also put the cookies in a plastic bag and crush them with a rolling pin.) You should have about 2 cups.

Turn crumbs into a medium-size bowl and mix with cinnamon. Stir in 2 tablespoons of the melted butter. Press crumbs firmly onto the bottom and side of a 10- or 10½-inch springform pan. Place in the refrigerator to chill while making the filling.

Preheat oven to 350°F.

Beat sugar and cream cheese together in a large bowl until light and fluffy. Beat in eggs one at a time. Add melted chocolate, vanilla, cocoa, and sour cream, beating constantly as you do so. Add remaining 8 tablespoons melted butter and blend thoroughly.

Bake on the lower oven rack for 45 to 50 minutes, or until the edge is completely set. The center of the cake may not appear to be set, but it will firm as the cake chills.

Cool cake until warm on a wire rack, then cover and refrigerate (still in the pan) for at least several hours or overnight before serving.

Remove cake from pan. You may prefer to just remove the side and leave the cake on the bottom of the springform pan to serve.

Garnish as your little chocolate-loving heart desires. I suggest lightly sweetened whipped cream topped with grated, semisweet chocolate.

MAKES 20 CONSERVATIVE SERVINGS.

Note: This cake keeps very well in the refrigerator for at least a week. Just be sure to keep it covered, and also be sure to chill the cake right away after serving from it.

Annie's Easy Chocolate Truffles

Luxurious chocolate truffles, the kind that come from ritzy little chocolate shops and cost nearly as much as the delicacy they resemble and for which they are named, are difficult to duplicate at home. Besides, unless these pricey truffles are impeccably fresh (made within the last 24 hours at the *most*), they are often not worth the money you spend for them. Better you should make *these* truffles. They are very rich and chocolatey, very melt-in-the-mouth, and very much less expensive. Just be sure to use the very best chocolate you can afford, and *do not* attempt to make truffles on a hot day or if the kitchen is very warm.

½ cup whipping cream
2 tablespoons butter, cut into small pieces
Pinch of salt
8 oz. semisweet chocolate, chopped into small pieces
Unsweetened cocoa powder for coating truffles

Combine cream, butter, and salt in a small saucepan. Bring to a simmer over medium heat. Adjust heat and simmer for 2 minutes. Remove from heat and cool to room temperature.

Melt chocolate in a small, heavy saucepan, stirring frequently, over *very low* heat. Remove from heat and cool to room temperature.

When chocolate has cooled, stir in cooled cream mixture until very smooth. Cover saucepan tightly with plastic wrap and chill for at least 4 hours before molding.

To mold truffles, first line a baking sheet with wax paper. Drop teaspoonfuls of the chocolate mixture onto the lined baking sheet and chill until firm.

Roll and press firm chocolate mixture into irregularly shaped, 1-inch balls between the palms of your hands. Chill again just until firm. Roll in cocoa powder to coat.

Truffles are best eaten right away, but will stay reasonably fresh for about one week if kept tightly wrapped in a very cool place.

MAKES ABOUT 2 DOZEN TRUFFLES.

Chocolate Pots

Of course these are really *pots de creme,* the upscale French dessert that should be served in small lidded cups. However, you can take my word for it that Chocolate Pots are fabulous, no matter what kind of downscale "pots" you choose to serve it in—Dixie cups will do— and tastes even better when eaten with demitasse spoons.

1 cup whipping cream
3 egg yolks
2 tablespoons sugar
Pinch of salt
1 package (6 oz.) semisweet chocolate pieces (1 cup)
1 teaspoon vanilla extract

Thoroughly mix cream, egg yolks, sugar, and salt in a heavy, medium-size saucepan. Set the saucepan over low heat and stir constantly until the mixture just begins to thicken, about 5 minutes. Remove from heat and immediately stir in chocolate and vanilla. Keep stirring until the chocolate is melted and the mixture is smooth.

Spoon into 6 chocolate pots, demitasse cups, or custard cups.

Chocolate pots may be served warm, at room temperature, or chilled.

MAKES 6 SERVINGS.

High-Class Chocolate Muffins

These muffins are *not* nursery food, so I suggest that you use the best semisweet chocolate you can lay your hands on and, for a really luxurious touch, cashew or macadamia nuts. To be most effective, eat at least one muffin while it's still warm from the oven, slathered with sweet, whipped butter.

9 oz. semisweet chocolate, chopped into small pieces
6 tablespoons butter
1½ cups all-purpose flour
1 teaspoon baking soda
¼ teaspoon salt
1 cup chopped nuts
⅔ cup sour cream
¼ cup light corn syrup
1 egg

Preheat oven to 375°F.

Place paper liners in 16 2½-inch muffin-pan cups and set aside.

Melt chocolate and butter in a heavy, medium-size saucepan, stirring frequently, over *very low* heat. Remove from heat and set aside to cool slightly.

Combine flour, baking powder, and salt in a large bowl. Add nuts and toss to coat thoroughly. Make a well in the center of the flour mixture and set aside.

Add sour cream, corn syrup, and egg to cooled chocolate mixture and stir until well blended. Scrape into the well in the flour mixture and stir just until moistened.

Spoon batter into muffin cups, filling each cup three-quarters full.

Bake for 15 to 18 minutes, or until a wooden pick inserted in the center comes out clean. Cool in pans for 5 minutes. Remove from pans and serve warm or cool completely.

MAKES 15 OR 16 MUFFINS.

Silky Black-and-White Terrine

I have paid as much as $10 for one slim slice of a luxurious terrine exactly like this one in many New York restaurants. This recipe makes two mini-loaf terrines, or one larger one. However, since the terrines have to be frozen anyway, two smaller ones are no problem, especially for the chocolate lover who owns two of these little loaf pans and who will love having a rich terrine on tap in the freezer for emergencies.

Chocolate terrines, you may have noticed, are almost always served in a "pool" of raspberry sauce, which is why I am suggesting an easy fresh strawberry sauce. (If you want to do the raspberry sauce it's simple enough: defrost a 10-oz. package of frozen raspberries in syrup and puree in a blender. Strain through a sieve to remove the seeds. That's it. One package will be enough for one small terrine. Double the recipe if you're making one large terrine.)

5 oz. white chocolate
15 oz. semisweet chocolate
4 tablespoons unsalted butter
1 cup whipping cream
1 teaspoon vanilla extract
A few strawberries and mint leaves for garnish

STRAWBERRY SAUCE:
½ pint strawberries, rinsed and hulled
3 tablespoons sugar

Butter two 5¾ x 3½ x 2-inch mini loaf pans (or one 8-inch loaf pan) and fit the bottoms with a piece of plastic film.

Melt white chocolate in a medium-size, heavy saucepan, stirring constantly, over *very low* heat. Divide between prepared loaf pans. Place pans in the freezer.

Melt semisweet chocolate and butter together in the same saucepan using the same method. Remove from heat and set aside to cool.

Whip cream with vanilla in a large, chilled mixing bowl until soft peaks form when beaters are lifted. Fold cooled chocolate into whipped cream in three stages.

Remove loaf pans from freezer. White chocolate should be firm. Spoon chocolate mixture into pans over white chocolate, dividing equally. Return pans to freezer and freeze until firm, about 3 hours.

To make sauce, place strawberries and sugar in the container of an electric blender and blend until as smooth as possible. Cover and chill until ready to assemble the dessert. This amount of sauce makes enough for four to six servings.

To unmold the terrines, dip pan bottoms in hot water for about 30 seconds. Tap pans to release terrines onto a work surface. If not serving immediately, leave plastic film in place. Place each terrine in a 1-quart plastic bag with a zipper top. Press out air, seal, and freeze until needed. Transfer terrine to the refrigerator for about 30 minutes to soften slightly before serving.

To serve, remove plastic film from white-chocolate layer and place terrine on a cutting surface. Using a hot, wet, serrated knife, cut each terrine into 8 slices.

Spoon chilled strawberry sauce in the bottom of four dessert plates. Arrange two slices of the terrine in each plate. Garnish with strawberry fans and mint leaves. (To make strawberry fans, lay one whole strawberry on its side. With a small, sharp knife, make several cuts through the strawberry, starting at the bottom, going up to the hull, but not through it. Press berry out, still attached at the hull, to make a fan.)

EACH SMALL TERRINE WILL SERVE FOUR CHOCOLATE FANCIERS. IF YOU LIKE YOU CAN CUT THE SLICES A LITTLE THINNER SO THAT EACH TERRINE WILL SERVE 6.

Chocolate-Syrup Cupcakes with Chocolate-and-Nuts Frosting

I suspect that this wonderful recipe may have originally come from those people who pack chocolate syrup and cocoa powder in little brown cans. By the way, my mother tells me that during World War II, when chocolate bars were scarcer than an eligible man, folks who lived in the area drove through Hershey, Pennsylvania just for a sniff of their favorite flavor.

4 tablespoons butter, softened
1/2 cup sugar
1/2 teaspoon vanilla extract
2 eggs
1 cup all-purpose flour
1/2 teaspoon baking soda
1/4 teaspoon baking powder
2/3 cup chocolate syrup

FROSTING:
4 tablespoons butter
1/4 cup unsweetened cocoa powder
2 to 2 1/2 cups confectioners' sugar
1/4 cup milk mixed with 1/2 teaspoon vanilla extract
1/2 cup (2 oz.) chopped walnuts or pecans

Preheat oven to 375°F.

Place paper liners in 16 2 1/2-inch muffin-pan cups and set aside.

Cream butter, sugar, and vanilla in a large bowl. Add eggs, one at a time, beating well after each addition.

Mix flour, baking soda, and baking powder in a medium-size bowl with a wire whisk until light and thoroughly blended. (Using a wire whisk to blend dry ingredients makes sifting unnecessary in this case.)

Add flour mixture alternately with chocolate syrup to the butter mixture until well blended.

Spoon batter into prepared muffin cups, filling each half full.

Bake for 20 to 25 minutes, or until a wooden pick inserted in the center of a few representative cupcakes comes out clean.

Place pans of cupcakes on wire racks to cool completely.

To make frosting, melt butter in a medium-size saucepan over medium-high heat. Stir in cocoa until smooth. Remove from heat. Add sugar and milk-and-vanilla mixture, alternately, beating until the mixture reaches a good spreading consistency.

Frost cooled cupcakes, using about 1 to 1½ tablespoons frosting for each cupcake. Lightly pat nuts onto tops of cupcakes.

MAKES ABOUT 16 CUPCAKES, AND ABOUT 1½ CUPS FROSTING.

Note: Cupcakes may be frozen, if you like. To freeze, set cupcakes on a baking sheet and place in the freezer just until the frosting is firm. Wrap cupcakes in foil or plastic film and freeze until the urge strikes.

Gummy Chocolate Sauce for Ice Cream

When poured warm over ice cream, this is the chocolate sauce that will harden slightly and become delightfully chewy as it cools. It's terrific spooned over just about any flavor of ice cream that you happen to have in the freezer, and if, at some point, you are forced to put on a "healthful" dessert show, you can spoon it over poached (or canned) pears, strawberries, raspberries, or orange segments, for example.

2 teaspoons butter
1 cup sugar
⅓ cup milk
1 oz. (1 square) unsweetened chocolate, broken in half
½ teaspoon vanilla extract

Melt butter in a 1 to 1½-quart saucepan. Remove from heat and add sugar, milk, and chocolate. Stir to combine. Place saucepan over medium heat and cook, stirring constantly, until chocolate melts and mixture comes to a hard boil.

Reduce heat and boil slowly, without stirring or otherwise disturbing, for about 5 minutes. Remove from heat and set aside to cool slightly. Beat in vanilla. Set the pan on the back of the stove or in some other reasonably warm location until you are ready to serve it.

Just before serving, stir sauce over medium-low heat, or just until quite warm, but not actually hot.

Spoon over ice cream (as cold as you can possibly scoop it) and serve immediately.

MAKES ABOUT 1 CUP SAUCE.

Note: If by some miracle there is leftover sauce, refrigerate it in a tightly covered container. Reheat it gently, stirring, or simply shove the container to the back of the refrigerator and treat yourself to a gummy spoonful or two whenever you need a chocolate high.

Anne Bailey's Chocolate Omelet

If you've ever eaten a flourless, chocolate cake (a rich, almost textureless cake that's actually a baked chocolate mousse, which could *only* have been created by a Frenchman), you know that it's every chocolate lover's dream come true—and a royal pain in the neck for the home baker. Annie's simple, but inspired, omelet tastes as good as any *gateau de mousse au chocolat* I've ever eaten, here or in France, and takes a mere thirty minutes from start to stomach.

1 tablespoon butter

6 oz. semisweet chocolate pieces (1 cup)

4 large eggs, separated

⅓ cup confectioners' sugar

⅓ cup sour cream

1 tablespoon orange or raspberry liqueur

Confectioners' sugar, for dusting omelet

SAUCE:

6 oz. semisweet chocolate pieces (1 cup)

⅔ cup whipping cream

2 tablespoons orange or raspberry liqueur

Preheat oven to 325°F.

Melt butter in a 10-inch, nonstick skillet with an ovenproof handle and set aside.

Melt chocolate in a small, heavy saucepan, stirring frequently, over *very low* heat. Remove from heat and set aside to cool.

While chocolate is cooling, beat egg whites in a large, grease-free bowl until frothy. Gradually beat in confectioners' sugar. Continue to beat until stiff peaks form when beaters are lifted.

Mix sour cream, egg yolks, and liqueur in a small bowl. Stir into cooled chocolate mixture until well blended. Gently fold this mixture into the beaten egg whites until no streaks of white remain. Scrape into prepared skillet, spreading gently to cover the bottom of the pan.

Place pan over low heat and cook *without stirring or otherwise disturbing* for 5 minutes. Transfer skillet to oven and bake for 15 to 18 minutes, or until a wooden pick inserted in the center comes out clean.

While omelet is baking, place chocolate and cream in a small, heavy saucepan. Cook over medium-low heat, stirring constantly, until the chocolate is melted. Remove from heat and set aside to cool. Stir in liqueur just before serving.

Remove omelet from oven and loosen around the edge with a small knife. Place a serving platter over the skillet and invert the omelet onto the platter. Sprinkle generously with confectioners' sugar.

Serve warm, cut into wedges, with chocolate sauce. Or chill both omelet and sauce and serve later.

MAKES 6 SERVINGS.

Aunt Ruth Chambers' Opera Fudge

My Aunt Ruth turns this fudge out perfectly every time. Perhaps it is because she simply does not know about the inherent hazards of candy-making in general, and fudge-making in particular, and so she doesn't worry about them. In order to avoid the pitfalls of graininess, fudge that is too hard, fudge that is too soft, and so on, my directions are several times as long as those on the neatly written recipe card Aunt Ruth gave me more than twenty years ago. This fudge is darker and richer (and a good deal more demanding) than Mamie's Fudge on page 169, more like the kind you buy in fudge shops at the seashore.

3 cups sugar
1 cup light cream or half-and-half
½ cup unsweetened cocoa powder
2 tablespoons light corn syrup
Pinch of salt
4 tablespoons butter
1 teaspoon vanilla extract

Generously butter a 9-inch square baking pan and set aside.

Butter the inside of a 3½- to 4-quart saucepan. Mix sugar, cream, cocoa, corn syrup, and salt in the prepared saucepan and set over medium heat. Cook, stirring constantly, until the sugar is dissolved and the mixture comes to a boil. (It is important that the sugar is dissolved before the mixture boils.) Lower heat and cover tightly. Cook, covered, for about 2 minutes, or until the steam created washes any lingering sugar crystals from the side of the pan. (One of the great mysteries of life is that if so much as one sugar crystal remains in the saucepan, it can cause a chain reaction that will turn the whole batch of fudge grainy.)

Uncover, place a candy thermometer in the saucepan and allow the fudge mixture to boil gently, without stirring, until the temperature on the thermometer reaches 238°F, or the soft-ball stage. This can take anywhere from 30 minutes to an hour. Be sure to watch carefully near the end.

Remove from heat and set on the kitchen counter. Leaving the thermometer in place, drop the butter into the fudge and simply allow it to melt undisturbed. When the fudge has cooled to 110°F (you should be able to place your hands comfortably on the bottom of the saucepan), at least 30 minutes, add the vanilla and beat relentlessly with a wooden spoon until the mixture begins to lose its gloss, holds its shape, and your arm feels ready to fall off. Turn into the prepared pan, *tout de suite,* as Aunt Ruth directs. (Do not attempt to scrape the chocolate that has hardened onto the side of the saucepan into the baking pan. Consequently, this is a great pan for licking.)

As soon as the fudge is firm, cut into squares and allow the fudge to finish cooling. If not to be eaten immediately (!), wrap pieces of fudge in plastic film or foil to preserve its soft, smooth texture.

MAKES ABOUT 1¾ POUNDS OF SOME OF THE MOST DELIGHTFUL FUDGE INTO WHICH YOU'VE EVER SUNK YOUR SWEET TOOTH.

All-Chocolate Sundae with Gooey Chocolate Sauce

Nothing shoos the blues like a good chocolate sundae made with two or three scoops of high-quality chocolate (page 191) or vanilla (page 39) ice cream, loaded with gooey chocolate sauce and chopped nuts, topped with a mound of *real* whipped cream and an otherwise revolting maraschino cherry. With the first spoonful of this fattening comfort food, close your eyes and picture yourself back at the cracked, marble soda-fountain counter in the corner drug store.

GOOEY CHOCOLATE SAUCE
1 package (6 oz.) semisweet chocolate pieces (1 cup)
½ cup light corn syrup
¼ cup light cream
1 tablespoon butter
¼ teaspoon vanilla extract

FOR EACH SUNDAE, YOU WILL NEED:
2 or 3 scoops chocolate ice cream (page 191)
4 or 5 tablespoons Gooey Chocolate Sauce (see note)
2 or 3 tablespoons chopped walnuts or pecans
¼ cup whipping cream, whipped
1 maraschino cherry

To make chocolate sauce, heat chocolate pieces with corn syrup in a small, heavy saucepan over low heat, stirring until blended. Stir in cream, butter, and vanilla. Continue stirring until butter has melted.

Serve warm or cooled. In a tall sundae glass, make layers of chocolate ice cream, Gooey Chocolate sauce, and nuts. Top with whipped cream and a maraschino cherry.

MAKES ABOUT 2¼ CUPS CHOCOLATE SAUCE.

Note: The chocolate sauce may be refrigerated in a tightly covered container until needed. Warm gently.

Chocolate Rocks

The ratio of peanut butter, raisins, and nuts to chocolate in these candies makes them fairly healthful, and they are certainly a snap to make. However, if you value your teeth, you will be sure to bring the "rocks" (or any chocolate, for that matter) to room temperature before eating, for they are accurately named.

1 package (12 oz.) semisweet chocolate pieces (2 cups)
1 cup crunchy peanut butter
1 cup dark raisins
1 cup salted or unsalted peanuts

Cover two baking sheets with wax paper and set aside.

Melt chocolate with peanut butter in the top of a double boiler over hot (not boiling) water. Stir in raisins and peanuts and remove from heat.

Drop by the spoonful (any size you like) onto prepared baking sheets. Chill until firm. Cover tightly and store in a cool place (the refrigerator is the best place in the summer), although long-term storage is rarely a problem.

MAKES ABOUT 2 POUNDS.

Frozen Chocolate Mousse Pie with a Buttery Chocolate Crust

To be shared by two or three, down-in-the dumps chocolate lovers who, alas, have nothing better to do on a Saturday night.

CRUST:

2 cups Oreo cookie crumbs (about 22 cookies)
⅓ cup melted butter

FILLING:

1 bar (4 oz.) semisweet chocolate
1 package (3 oz.) cream cheese, softened
½ cup confectioners' sugar
2 eggs
½ teaspoon vanilla extract
½ pint whipping cream
Unsweetened whipped cream and chocolate curls or grated chocolate, for garnish

Prehat oven to 375°F.

To make crust, mix cookie crumb with melted butter. Turn mixture into a 9-inch pie pan lined with aluminum foil, pressing mixture over bottom and side evenly to form a shell. Place in the freezer while preparing filling.

To make filling, melt chocolate in a small, heavy saucepan, stirring frequently, over *very low* heat. Set aside to cool to lukewarm.

Beat cream cheese and confectioners' sugar in a medium-size bowl until creamy. Beat in eggs and vanilla until mixture is well blended. Add cooled chocolate and stir until combined.

Beat cream in a large bowl until soft peaks form when beaters are lifted.

Fold chocolate mixture, a third at a time, into whipped cream. Remove pie pan from freezer. Carefully lift shell out of pan and discard foil. Return crust to pan. Spoon chocolate mixture into prepared pie shell, smoothing the top lightly with a wide spatula or the back of a large spoon. Freeze until firm, about 3 hours.

To serve, thaw slightly and cut into wedges. Garnish with whipped cream, sprinkled with chocolate curls or grated chocolate.

MAKES 4 TO 6 GENEROUS SERVINGS.

The Ultimate Chocolate Ice Cream

And I do mean *ultimate*. This chocolate ice cream doesn't stint on any of the rich ingredients always associated with old-fashioned ice cream, before we started worrying about cholesterol, saturated fats, and sugar. Like most ice cream, it's best if eaten after it has had a chance to languish in the freezer for a day or so (or at least a few hours)—if you can stand it.

> *1 bar (4 oz.) semisweet chocolate*
> *1 pint half-and-half*
> *¾ cup sugar*
> *2 tablespoons all-purpose flour*
> *3 eggs, well beaten*
> *1½ cups whipping cream*
> *2 teaspoons vanilla extract*

Combine chocolate and half-and-half in a heavy, 3-quart saucepan. Cook over medium-low heat, stirring occasionally, until chocolate is melted.

Mix sugar and flour in a small bowl and stir into chocolate mixture. Cook over medium heat, stirring, just until mixture begins to boil when you stop stirring. Stir a small amount of the hot chocolate mixture into the eggs, then rapidly stir eggs into the hot chocolate mixture with a wire whisk. Continue to cook, whisking constantly, until mixture thickens. Remove from heat. Place chocolate mixture, still in the saucepan, in the refrigerator to chill. When cold, stir in whipping cream and vanilla.

Pour cold chocolate mixture into the canister of an ice cream maker and freeze according to the manufacturer's directions.

Scrape ice cream into one or two freezer containers with tight fitting lids, leaving about ½-inch headspace. Cover and place in the freezer for a day or two to ripen.

MAKES ABOUT 2 PINTS.

Chocolate Waffles with Chocolate-Pecan Sauce

Under normal circumstances these would be considered a dessert waffle. However, the chocolate addict in a depressed state will eat them at any time of the day or night with plenty of chocolate sauce. Other toppings to be considered are: whipped cream, ice cream, sweetened berries, hard sauce, foamy sauce, other sundae toppings, or just plain confectioners' sugar.

2 squares (1 oz. each) unsweetened baking chocolate
1½ cups all-purpose flour
1 tablespoon baking powder
¼ teaspoon salt
3 eggs, separated
¼ cup solid white vegetable shortening
⅔ cup sugar
1¼ cups milk
½ teaspoon vanilla extract
½ cup finely chopped pecans

SAUCE:
1 recipe Gooey Chocolate Sauce (page 188)
½ cup finely chopped pecans

Melt chocolate in a small, heavy saucepan, stirring frequently, over *very low* heat. Remove from heat and set aside to cool.

Combine flour, baking powder, and salt in a medium bowl and set aside.

Beat egg whites in the large grease-free bowl of an electric mixer until stiff peaks form when beaters are lifted. Gently scrape beaten whites into another bowl and set aside.

In the same large bowl of the electric mixer (no need to wash), cream shortening and sugar until light and fluffy. Beat in cooled chocolate and egg yolks until thoroughly blended. Beat in milk alternately with flour mixture. Stir in vanilla and nuts. Gently fold egg whites into batter until no streaks of white remain.

Bake in a preheated waffle maker according to manufacturer's directions. (One-half cup of batter will yield one 6½-inch waffle.)

Stir pecans into warm Gooey Chocolate Sauce and serve with waffles.

MAKES TEN 6½-INCH WAFFLES, ABOUT 2½ CUPS SAUCE.

INDEX